JUNE

Nogginers

Nogginers

Paul Kestell

BLACK CORMORANT BOOKS
DUBLIN

Published by Black Cormorant Books
© Paul Kestell, 2016

ISBN: 978-1530639502

Contents

AUTHOR'S NOTE   VII

The Messenger Boy   1

Workers   11

Frogs   25

Visits   39

Blood   55

Hate Lessons   67

The Posh Party   93

David's Room   119

Betty Drew   135

Weekly with Mrs Tims   153

Corpus Christi   163

Leaving   171

Author's Note

Whilst every effort has been made to be accurate, my memory is not what it once was so you will forgive me if I got a few things wrong, whether it be place names or events or the years they took place. Most of the things in these stories happened in some form or another between the years outlined. However, none of them happened exactly the way I have described them or to the characters I have created.

This is volume one of what I hope to be three volumes of stories set in Sallynoggin where I grew up. I hope I represent us little Nogginers well, without patronising anyone or the area itself. Suffice to say that we had our own version of the English language: I use words like lanch or lanched, which means holding on with your hands whilst dropping from a height; or the word belled, as in 'He belled it,' meaning diving through the air – this derives from the term belly-flop. I refer to the ring, but the ring wasn't circular, it was a triangular grassy area; and, finally, Gay Byrne is an Irish TV presenter and celebrity.

The Messenger Boy

1968

Molly Kingston made a face at him as he passed; she ran into the shelter of the concrete porch that divided the houses and she called out.

When he looked around she had retreated a little so as he could just about see her. 'Yer bike is shite, young Seanie.' He saw her pale face recede to the shadows.

'It's way better than yers,' he shouted.

Knowing that she didn't have a bike and possibly never would.

'Seen yah blow up yer tires wit yer mouth – it's so fuckin big.'

When he looked around the porch was a dirty grey; he knew that she stood in that space watching him. He fumbled the bike out the narrow gate, catching the front spokes in a piece of wire protruding from the railings.

'Watch yah don't go over the handlebars – yah dat had

de yellow jam jars.' Seanie wondered why she called yellow jaundice 'yellow jam jars'.

It took a minute to free the wire from the spokes; he was annoyed because it meant that he could still hear her.

'Yer a skinny mallink – an yer da's a brutal singer an yer sisters ar snobs.'

'Shut up, you!' Seanie cried out to her.

'I won't, who da fuck dah yah tink yer talkin ta?'

She appeared once more but this time he froze; she had done something to her hair. Standing sideways she came out of the shadows, she all golden with strands of brown curls cradling her emerging breasts. She stayed that way so he could see her strong behind, the high ridge of her tummy making a tiny shadow on the wall. 'Be careful, yah don't wanna get de yellow jam jars again; yah lucked shite!'

He managed to move the bike through the gate.

The earth over the kerb was hard brown and dotted with puddles. Someone had deposited two large stones into the biggest pool. The water ran fast around them.

He imagined Molly Kingston shouting, 'Beware of de rapads,' as he floated around the stones on an abandoned lollypop stick – with one giant surge the stick was forced to the bottom. Marooned, she became miniature, diving into the rapids to save him. This was her way of proving her true love.

In truth she had been very kind to him during his bout of yellow jaundice. When his body constricted he hadn't the strength to drink a cup of water. She came to visit him and her ma had scrubbed her, just to spruce her up. That was the first time he saw her eyes clearly – all the good sapping from them – he could tell she was full of vitamins, like the sun.

The day itself was cosying to the low light after the heavy rain of the morning. He watched as people alighted from the bus, wearing dark colours to suit the mood. The sky was low and thick with mesh; the true colours were elsewhere.

The footpath twisted outside of Drews' gate, the one they shared with Durkans. The path was a different shade here – it was clear white by the hydrant, where the older fellas used to play dab. They would toss coins to the hydrant; once in they became a killer and if you tossed your coin onto another lad's coin then you won it. He was no use at dab. Anytime he tried it he lost. It seems the older fellas played it a lot because they were so good at it, but lads his own age avoided it.

He noticed the rainwater dripping slowly from the dull leaves of Durkans' hedge, wetting the foundation of the rail that was buried within it. He was thinking that it's a long road now: to go 10,000 miles in six inches, not forgetting that he was riding a supersonic bike.

Lambkin's dog chased him, Shadow Lambkin chasing his bike; he doing a million miles an hour over fast terrain. Shadow would nip at your heels but that was the extent of it. He got bored easily too; a bus taking off at the terminus distracted him. So he stopped chasing the bike, and he went to chase the bus instead. He was all low, prancing through the grass like a sheepdog, only to emerge a rabid wolf. Then the bus conductor taunting him by lashing his ticket-machine belt against the platform.

Shadow went ballistic; every dog around the place came charging after him. One bus conductor with a belt; ten dogs rampaging up the street.

The bike went flying round Smyth's Corner. Their van was gone from the driveway – old man Smyth was away collecting eggs. He came by on Friday evenings, then his daughter called on Wednesdays to collect the money. He used to have a green van but now he drove a blue one that didn't look any newer. The garden looked bare without it. They were the first to knock through the railings and cement a driveway.

Seanie was distracted as Mrs Martin from across the street came down the garden path, her brolly full up against just a few drops of rain. The dogs were charging home; the chase was over. Now the pack dissolved into threes and twos, ending in ones as each dog made for home. Mrs Martin stopped and undid her umbrella. She looked towards her house, checking if she had left something behind. Seanie rode on, thinking of trays of eggs; the dark night's opening the door to the slight female hand waiting to be paid. How his ma always made sure that he had the money ready. They were good eggs, too – his ma said they must be good hens. His ma knows about hens; she kept hens when she was growing up. Which was great because she never had to buy an egg. Eggs were very important, so good for you.

He checked to see if Jill Macken was looking out her window. She had a habit of peering out from her upstairs window on wet days. But she wasn't there. All he could see was a dismal pulled curtain. Seanie liked Jill Macken because her blush painted her rodent-shaped face to the point of embarrassment, yet all was saved by her shoulder-length hair, stroking her wide shoulders.

He wondered did she mind living next door to the bachelors, the bald men whose only boast was the luxury of Christmas dinner in the Victor Hotel. Odd for two brothers to live together. They were midsized middle-aged bachelors, with a penchant for entertaining kids in their garden. He took the corner at a million miles per hour. He had covered a million miles in three revolutions of the wheel. The people down below were ant-like; his supersonic bike cruised over them.

The main road to the shops was empty so it was megaspeed up the hill, before sighting the big yellow church. It stood as a palace, impaling all below it to the flat landscape.

Was that him? His father racing up the street. The American aunt of a family friend stops him to congratulate him on his singing. His father takes it well, a mixture of glee and embarrassment, but mostly glee. She bangs him on the shoulder, telling him how fantastic he is. Seanie holds his hand; he is worried for him with this attention. His father is a quiet man, unused to praise of any sort.

'Genius sheer genius,' she says. 'In all my years. I have never heard anything quite like that. "King of Kings and Lord of Lords / King of Kings and Lord of Lords / and he shall reign forever and ever / forever and ever / Halleluiah Halleluiah.'"

Handel's Messiah, his ma informs him, was first performed in Dublin's Fishamble Street. Wow – this woman from Chicago wants to kiss his da because he was the lead tenor in the church choir. She kisses him twice; she tells him he is a genius and fabulous. But his ma never said that his father was a genius, or brilliant. No, she put the whole thing down to yer man Handel. 'Halleluiah Halleluiah.'

Seanie crossed the road and straight away came to the houses of some respectable people. The Nolans and the Sullivans – both very respectable families; their houses were immaculate. The front windows neatly painted white, the gardens trimmed along with impressive flower arrangements. Manicured knee-high hedgerows ran between the houses – they were exactly the same save for the Sullivans didn't have the hedgerow on the other side, instead they had a line of roses pressed against the garden path. Mr Sullivan was coming out of his gate.

'Hello, son,' he said, stooping to look over at Seanie.

'Hello, Mr Sullivan,' Seanie said respectfully.

'How is yer father?'

'Not bad, he is alright save for his stomach is a bit queer.'

'That sounds bad enough, is he takin bread soda?'

'Yeah, he's tried everythin but nuthin works. I'm goin to Cleary's to see if I can get him this new stuff – everyone swears by it.'

'What's that now?'

'Maalox.'

'Maalox?'

'Yeah, it's new out,' Seanie said knowingly.

'I must remember that name, son. I have a few problems myself – tell your daddy we miss him in the choir – tell him I said he is to get better soon.'

'I will,' Seanie said; the bike returned to speed over vast continents.

Seanie was thinking about Mr Sullivan, the story he told about the dead sheep. His ma always said that he was a very respectable man, very quiet-spoken but reserved. He was, for sure: didn't Seanie's sisters go to play canasta in Sullivans' house with the Sullivan boys once a week? Canasta was a posh game and anyone who played it was well-heeled by association.

Mr Sullivan worked for the Post and Telegraphs and one day they were erecting a line of poles by a ditch. All was going well but suddenly they encountered a fierce problem sinking one pole into the ground. On further investigation wasn't there a dead sheep buried just where they wanted to lodge the pole. This was Mr Sullivan's story; now it wasn't much of a story but it got Seanie thinking about poles and about dead sheep, and he remembered it over and over.

Mrs Cleary was a very good-looking woman with long dark hair draping over her shoulders. She was behind the counter chatting to this oul wan and they were talking about summer holidays and bumper cars. Mrs Cleary was reminiscing about her holiday by the sea and the oul wan just agreeing with her all the time. Seanie wondered with the state of the oul wan maybe had she never been on holiday, and if so would she have ever got into a bumper car?

'Can I help you?' Mrs Cleary said kindly.

'I need a bottle of Maalox – it's for my da!'

'Maalox – I'll have a look but I'm not sure we have it. I've heard of it alright but I dunno if they sent it in to us yet.' And she was gone searching and the oul wan, abandoned, smiled at Seanie, who cheekily smiled back at her.

'I'll see ya missus!' the oul wan shouted, but Mrs Cleary had slipped out the back and the oul wan left disappointed. The door chimed when she opened it, and then it chimed again because she caught the sleeve of her coat in it so she had to reopen and then close it again.

'I have it. We just got it in this mornin.' Mrs Cleary beamed. 'There you go, it's dear enough,' she added apologetically, so Seanie gave her his money, and he felt bad as it had taken his mother and father an age to decide about spending it on the Maalox.

On the way home the street was quiet and the church bell sounded behind him. He knew there must be a funeral coming for half-past five as it was too early for the Angelus.

Seanie rode all over the world and crossed the road outside of Nolans'. Once again he admired the stillness and perfection of Sullivans' house. Freewheeling down the hill with the black garden rails flashing by, he noticed a young girl with jet-black hair playing in her garden; she was doing handstands. It was nothing much, her white frock falling down allowing a glimpse of her frilly white

8

knickers for just a second before she stood up again. Seanie wanted to stop the bike just to see if she would do it again. But his common sense prevailed and he went on, around the corner by the dark mongrel hedges.

Sliding off the edge of the world before he passed the bachelor boys, and once more he searched for Jill Macken but once again she was nowhere to be seen. The egg van was back in Smyths' driveway, and as he rode on the rain started to fall. Huge individual thick dark drops wet his head as he cycled by Drews'.

The church bell sounded once more; he eased the bike through the gate. He was heading on to the porch. There in the darkness Molly Kingston hid.

'Yahs think yahs are great with yer posh sisters playin canasta!'

'Shut up, Molly!' Seanie screamed at her.

'An yer oul lad is a brutal singer – he can't sing a note!'

'Yeah an wat can you do?' Seanie cried.

And Molly was gone again; she melded into the flashes of light stirring from the clouds over the backyard. The bike wobbled. Seanie just about saved it; he hit the hard wall, on his right side. When in the yard he saw the white liquid turn blue; it seeped through his pocket. He tried desperately to seal the broken jar but the contents spilled out without mercy.

'You bloody eejit,' his ma said. 'That was the last few bob we had – how could you be so stupid?'

'It was an accident,' Seanie said, glancing at his da, who looked pale and weak.

'Never mind,' his father said, 'these things happen.'

Workers

1969

I look at Ben with envy, knowing he is younger than me by almost two years. Ben hasn't quite got there yet, unlike me he has no budding problems with pores; I have greasy skin and I am plagued by the arrival of these ugly spots on my chin, but Ben has perfect skin and perfect curls and I am envious as the more he grows the better looking he becomes. Gone are the days when his mother packed him off to the pictures with his head soaked in hair oil, yet I think it made him look sophisticated, much older, more like a man than a boy.

When I look at him all the memories of ducking and diving behind the curtains in the Pavilion Cinema come rushing back. Ben isn't the worst of them either – Massey probably acts the toughest, but that's because he's a bit stupid rather than malicious – and then I go through the thick curtains to the sudden darkness: one, two, three grab me, and they push me to the floor, giving me phantom digs. Laughing, I emerge into the light where rows of framed photographs of Hollywood stars decorate the walls. We go on to the toilets and Massey is the proudest, he claims the most digs; he takes to standing up straight to make himself taller whilst taking a pee. I like Massey because he's robust and fair and he's an adventurer and he comes out with some good ones like, 'When I was down in the jungle,' whatever that means. But it is great as it makes me think about Tarzan and dastardly poachers. Ben's fond of him too so we always include Massey when others won't but sometimes he just isn't around, he has better things to do and he's a divil for bad company.

It is exactly an hour since Ben's older brother Frank tickles him till he wets himself; now there isn't much pee, barely enough to blot the front of his shorts, but no matter Ben has to change into longers. Frank does it to him regularly, tickling him without mercy till Ben's frantic cries become screams and then he wriggles and tries to roll, but Frank pins his shoulders fast with his knees. Ben is never embarrassed about the pee, he takes it all in his stride and Frank doesn't seem to care too much either; he just goes on about his business. laughing to himself.

We decide to go to explore the fields beyond the church because Frank tells us about the big old ruined house and how people say that it was burned down because it is haunted. Anyway all of that area is in vogue lately as the legend of 'the woman with the pig's head' was fresh in everyone's mind. There was a right furore, as the rabble gather at the edge of the wood. Then someone shouts out, 'There she is!' and the crowd retreats, but we take advantage and make our way to the front. I don't see a thing, but Ben being Ben swears he sees her taking cover behind a tree trunk. I pester him to tell me what she looks like.

'She is like a woman wit de head of a pig.' he says. I feign horror and he is very happy that I join in the drama, but really I have my suspicions about the whole thing and then I am sure that Ben is just winding me up.

'Yah can shave 'em off.'

'Wat?' I say back to him.

'De spots, shave them off, can't yah?'

'Wat about de blood?'

'Dunno, looks like deyed cum off wit a razor.'

I imagine the blood soaking my skin with these detached spots in the palm of my hand.

'Nah, Ben, too bloody.'

I think he accepts it as he goes quiet, but then he says, 'Mary got 'em but she can't shave.'

I am thinking of his sister and how dark she is and I didn't know that she had spots. Mary is big and heavy but she has a beautiful face and I always think that her skin is perfect as it sticks fast to her jaw.

'Dey went away on der own!' Ben announces.

I see the oul wans walking up the street, they are Mrs this and Mrs that, and I am amused as they don't know me from Adam, but I know one of them. The Noggin is funny like that as you get to know loads of people so counting houses one, two, three, I miss four and five, hey I am good again for six and seven and eight, I know it is Mrs Harte and some other oul wan carry straw shopping bags. Mrs Harte looks like a cow because her clothes are stuck to her like leather, she is thin at the front going up, but really fat and sticky out at the rear, and her hips carry out her bottom at least a foot, yet she is tall with it so she leans over the other oul wan. She smiles over at Ben and me and in fairness I'd say she smiles at all the younger ones as she passes.

We are nearly at the Old Folks Centre and Ben wants to go over to the green opposite the shops. We go and we sit there on the kerb like hards with me looking up at the church; as expected, all is quiet at this time of the day, and the sun beats off the bonnet of a car that someone abandoned in the church car park.

Ben says, 'Wat yah tink of us smokin?'

I am distracted by the bus thundering up the road; it beats hard against the pavement when stopping to let people off.

I go, 'I'll choke, Ben – do yah wan me to choke?'

'Yah won't choke!' Ben assures me, 'Sure me da smokes sixty a day.'

'He be good at it,' I say. 'Do yah tink we look hard sittin here?'

Ben was thinking about it, but then he starts counting his money, and he counts it twice.

'It's not wher yah sit dat makes yah hard.'

'But all de hards sit here,' I say, and Ben puts his money back in his pocket.

'Silkcut or No. 6?'

'De ad for No. 6 is deadly, all dose fellas divin inta de pool.'

'Mus be great swimmers,' Ben says. 'Dah yah tink Doukie Davis is hard?'

'He looks it!' Ben takes his money out again and the bus passing is very noisy so I can barely hear him.

'Don't tink he's as hard as Paddy Mac.'

I don't know so I just say, 'Doukie looks hard to me.'

'The oul wan in Arnold's won't give nuthin.' The change went back in Ben's pocket.

'She tinks bad of givin me de civil war chewin gum!'

Ben laughs and says, 'Dat's bad, bur she's a wurse chin dan yah – she gotta beard now … Peter Kiely will give yah cigarettes if yah say it's far yer da or yer ma!'

'Long as we don't get de oul lady?'

'Nah, she'll be out the back.' We are on our feet and now I'm counting my money.

'Will yah ask?' Ben says, moving on as I follow.

'I will not, yer de one dat knows about smokin!' Ben smiles back at me as we cross over to the shops and by the line of multi-coloured pillars.

Kiely's is dark and Peter is up a ladder at the biscuit tins. Ben starts to read the ice cream stickers on the side of the fridge. The old lady is peeping out from the back door; it is like she wants to make herself useful, but the shop isn't busy. Peter comes down from the ladder. He moves briskly around the counter to the weighing scales. A young girl on an errand waits patiently for her paper bag of Kimberly and Coconut Creams, then Ben gets brave leaning arrogantly on the counter, his elbows stuck out.

'Gentlemen?' Peter Kiely turns his gaze towards us. The girl leaves, noisily pushing her paper bag into her shopping bag.

'Huw yah, Peter?' Ben says. I go red and take a step back; I want to go and study the ice-cream stickers again, and pretend that I was uninterested in the proceedings, but it was all too late for that.

'Can I get two No. 6 an a box of matches?' Ben was good – he sounded really professional.

'Der far me ma,' Ben explains. 'She has nerves,' he adds unnecessarily.

'I can't,' says Peter apologetically. 'I only have Silkcut open. I don't want to be opening No. 6 as people usually buy ten at a time.'

Ben looks at me like he needs guidance and I just feel like running out into the sun. I start to panic and wonder why we are doing this to ourselves – bloody cigarettes that I will choke on for sure.

'De Silkcut will do her!' Ben says knowledgeably, 'Her nerves won't know no difference.' Peter goes to get the fags, smiling.

'They are for your ma now?' he asks, putting the loose cigarettes down, and then he reaches back to the shelf for the box of matches.

'Ah yeah, dey are.' Ben says; he pays the money and out we walk.

'Yah owe me sixpence.'

I'm about to argue but there's no sense in that, I just give him sixpence and he takes it, laughing.

'Yah wer terrible, you look so guilty – I was tinkin he wus goin to say no!'

'Well he didn't, did he?'

Ben hands me my fag and I nearly crush it, such is the hold I have on it; I watch as he stoops down by the church wall and strikes a match.

'Inhale,' he says, and I do. Then I choke, cough and splutter.

He finds it strong too but he is much better than me, he leads the way and we climb through a gap in the hedge into the field. I am still coughing and Ben is walking ahead. He stops to take another pull and he says, 'Inhale,' and this time I don't cough but I don't like the tarry taste either. Mine burned down quick enough, but there is something cool about throwing away a butt.

Ben makes a big deal out of the last pull on his fag, exhaling smoke through his nose as well as his mouth. 'I am goin to take it up,' he says, 'it's the craic.'

'Nah – not far me.' I was thinking of ball and keeping fit and the like.

Ben didn't seem to mind me not smoking, in the end I suppose he just realised that I wasn't any good at it.

We walk on behind the old ruins into the next field when suddenly we hear shouting and roaring and through a gap in the hedge we see the girls from Hillcourt playing hockey. We stay quiet as we look at the girls charging around in a fiercely contested game. The excitement in seeing the action settles us into watching the match. A blonde girl gets a right bash on the shins but she plays on bravely and then she exacts revenge on her opponent, tapping her ankles with her stick as the girl makes a break for it. When the girl turns around to protest she then gets a bang in the ribs for her trouble. Then Hillcourt score a goal and all hell breaks loose – players and mentors all converge on the goal scorer – we felt like joining in!

'Der all prods – all of 'em, posh prods,' Ben says.

'Good players though,' I say back.

'I give yah dat,' Ben says as we move away.

I am sorry we are going as the girls were luscious and I think of Massey, he loves girls, and he is missing this just to hang around with the hards, up to no good, God knows what they'd be up to. Then I wish I was posh so as I could see these girls all of the time, I'd love to be in with them, and I really want to be one of their friends. We leave the blue-green hockey players and cross the fields and Ben is idling in front. He stops for a moment to wipe the sweat from his brow.

'Bloody hot, I hate de heat!'

'Hate de heat?'

'Yeah, it saps me energy.'

'We can rest over by de ruins.'

'Hope ders no ghosts.' Ben was moving on again.

'Wat if it's a mirage?'

'I wunder wat it's like to 've a mirage?'

'Dunno,' Ben says. 'Yah will be seein hoc,
chargin at yah, mus be dreadful dough – to see
palm trees, an go chargin an der be nuthin der!'

'Suppose yah jus roll about in de sand till yah die.'

The ruins are massive up close – thick clusters of ivy grow
out of dark holes, all of the side walls have crumbled and
I see the remains of an old fireplace. The stairs have fallen
down, and broken bricks are heaped on each other; there
are just two steps of the stairs still intact near the top,
but the landings all caved in, and beyond that steel wire
sticks out randomly from the walls. Upstairs windows are
invaded by the branches of trees, and underneath there are
pockets of moss stuck in the cracks of the outer walls. The
entrance is small but it was once much bigger as the rubble
has squashed it all down.

I want to speak but Ben hushes me. In the narrow room
adjoining, smoke billows through the wide window space.
We can't see in there. The smoke gets thicker as it changes
from white to black so Ben moves carefully as the floor is
uneven with loose stones and broken slates.

I follow and realise that we are making lots of noise and
then I slip but, grabbing Ben's shoulder, he takes my weight.

There he is, sitting with his back to us, and we both recog-
nise him immediately. Paddy Mac, his long locks a giveaway,
the old jacket from the 'good suit' that he always wears. He
is melting lead, his right hand protected by an old glove,

rtled and turns around in terror;
ιe doesn't know me. The blood

sneakin up on me.'
'Wat yah burnin?' Ben says
winking.
..y Mac goes.

Go on ta fuck.' Paddy Mac is moving sacks away from the flames; he has way more sacks scattered around the fire. 'Did yah get it on de church roof?' Ben sits down on a concrete block just to get a closer look; it is roasting everywhere and the fire is throwing out unreal heat.

'Fuck off wit yahs!' Paddy Mac looks at me. I am inclined to fuck off now but Ben ignores him.

'Huw dah yah ger up on de roof?'

'It's not off de church, dis roof fell in!' Ben smiles at Paddy Mac, who eyes me funny. It's like he is happy to have Ben for company and amusement but he isn't so sure about me. 'Don't believe yah,' Ben says. 'Lead falls down far yah Paddy, like its rainin gold hey!'

'Funny,' says Paddy, 'havin a penny, I melt dis down an I get a few bob in Dunleary after!'

'Dey pay yah far dis?' Ben asks like he has just discovered a great source of income.

Paddy snarls, ''Ave yis cigarettes?'

'Nah,' Bens says, 'only matches.'

'Gis de matches.' Ben reaches into his jeans pocket and he retrieves his box of matches and gives them to Paddy. Paddy in turn reaches into the inside pocket of his jacket. He takes out a tiny butt. There is very little left on it but he tears off a piece of a brown paper bag lying beside him. He takes a light from the fire whilst leaving our box of matches idle on bit of a brick. It burns the end of the butt. I want to ask him why he doesn't use the matches, but then I change my mind. 'Yis can carry dis over ta de bus; give yah a few bob?'

'I dunno, Paddy,' Ben says, like he is losing interest. 'It'll be very heavy, haw much far us?'

'Two bob each.'

'Yer broke,' I say. Paddy seems annoyed by me – it is like he only negotiates through Ben.

'Two bob, wen I sell 'em.'

'How'll we get paid?' I am arrogant now. Ben stays quiet to see what Paddy has to say about it.

'Back in a few hours – wait at de terminus, won't fuckin let yah down; I swear.'

It takes ages; Paddy Mac has to let the lead cool and we leave him to his work. Ben wants to go back to the shops to buy more fags but I talk him out of it, so we sit on the grass looking up at the ruined shell of the old house.

'Dah yah tink it wus a hotel?' Ben says.

'Nah – the 'Benburb' was a hotel!'

'Wat yah tink it wus?'

'Dunno – jus a big house – maybe a farmhouse.'

'Wunder haw it burnt down?' Ben is looking at the remains of Paddy's smoke. The fire's almost out; I can tell because it hits the air in a straight line blowing white with tiny black tails attached.

We carry Paddy's sacks of lead. Mine is heavy but Ben's is worse and in fairness to Paddy he labours with his as well. We pass them from one to the other as we climb through hedges and over a narrow ditch with trickles of muddy water.

'Not messin lads – I will see yah at de terminus – wud never've gotta dis over on me own – so we split de profits, eh!'

We watch the bus leave and Paddy sits downstairs to keep an eye on his stash. Ben wants to buy another fag but I talk him into buying sweets. We have enough for two bags of acid drops. We walk back up the road towards the Pigs Fields and Ben is quiet; he is lost in his own thoughts. I notice how sturdy he is now compared to what he used to be, but I mourn for my own strength, as I seem to mature only with oily skin and spots: I feel my legs getting stronger and my torso stretch, but my arms are still so thin and they ache from carrying the bags of lead. Ben seems alright, though, and he isn't complaining at all.

'What dos Massey meen wen he says down in de jungle?'

'Dunno,' I say and I didn't. I say, 'He says funny tings all de time like, he says stupid tings like "Tings are lookin black in Africa."'

'I don't get dat either,' Ben says sadly. We arrive in his garden and he falls down out of habit.

'Will I get a ball?'

'Nah,' Bens goes, 'we 'ave to keep an eye far Paddy.'

A 58 and a 7a come in to the terminus; he's not on either of them.

'You wudn't know wit 'em,' Ben says, looking at the foreign students walking from the bus, by the garden hedge. 'I don't mind 'em, bur on de bus, de one in de front seat wans to talk wit de wan in de back seat.'

I agree and add, 'Der moths ar nice dough.'

Ben laughs and then he spies Billyo Doyle the far side of the street. He is walking home gaily from his employment. Billyo is tall and lean; he is good-looking but that is negated by his unusual height, and the fact that he still wears a blue overall with 'Lourdes Hospital' embroidered on it.

'Ah Billyo, yer a big bollocks.'

Billyo stops in his tracks, 'Fuck yah, Ben Mooney, yer not goin to rise me dis time.'

'Yer a big baby!' Ben shouts; Billyo keeps walking, pretending not to hear him.

'Yer only a big baby Billyo – Mammy's boy – big baby!'

Billyo snaps and the chase is on. He legs it across the street. Ben is gone like a flash. Billyo is in the garden and Ben jumps the dividing hedge into Murphy's. Billyo jumps it like a hurdler, and Ben twists and turns like a scrum half. Ben makes it to Murphy's back door with seconds to spare. He leaps onto the wooden frame and bunts himself up just out of reach of Billyo's marauding hand.

'I'll kill you, Mooney!' Billyo says, looking at me. He retreats slowly just in case Ben reappears from over Murphy's back wall.

'Yer a big baby, Billyo!' Bens shouts from the safety of the backyard. Billyo departs and he seems satisfied with himself like he's proud of the chase. Ben reappears through his own back gate, checking to make sure Billyo is gone.

A bus pulls in. We walk down to the corner of the garden to inspect the passengers. There he is, Paddy Mac. The last one to get off, he is bagless and he walks funny like he has drink taken.

"Ave yah got ar few bob?' Ben asks as he passes.

Paddy looks at us incredulously like he is trying to make out who we are.

'Got fuck all for it – wasn't worth de carry.'

Ben let him have it. 'Tah fuck, Paddy; yah promised us!'

Paddy wiped his mouth with the sleeve of his 'good suit' jacket.

'Go fuck yerselves,' and off he went.

Frogs

1970

Things that Massey did that entered local folklore: on a Christmas morning he ran around the ring in his nude and then, as he was a divil for bad company, he got into robbing houses up in Granitefield ... his only saving grace was that he was teaching his fellow miscreants to read English, by reading from his comics up in the woods. So his ma said to Mrs Mooney, and Mrs Mooney thought it so funny she told my ma ... and thus it became a regular joke.

The good thing about Massey was his sense of innocence and humour. He had no idea that folk thought him funny, or odd ... he acted like everything he did was normal and if anything he touched on arrogance, like if people didn't adhere to his doctrine, well then they were out of step, not he. He ran around the ring in his nude for a dare with his younger brother Edward ... he robbed houses because Shorty Kennedy asked him to do look out and he just couldn't say no to Shorty, who at the time held the status of a mafia don.

The reading from his comics was just his philanthropic self coming to the fore – it was like he was announcing to all the world one simple fact that bigger fucking eejits than him existed. It was his job not only to educate these miscreants but to introduce them to the wonderful genre of the *Beano*, *Dandy*, *Hotspur*, and *Lion*, and his own personal favourite, the *Valiant*. Massey had no time for the more sophisticated publications from Dell, titles like *Superman* or *Spiderman* – they were too fanciful and violent for his taste – and the truth was he was more likely to engage in swaps with my kid brother than stand at the front door with my older brother going 'have, have, seen it, have, have, don't want'. That operation was lightning fast with covers turning over in the style that a good teller counts bank notes.

Ben Mooney was fond of Massey; I guess he enjoyed his wildness, but perhaps it was his simple childishness that Ben liked the most. One day we set off, the three of us, accompanied by my kid brother Liam. I suppose this wouldn't normally have induced any true excitement, save for Liam was only seven he was four years younger than me – and it was our first time bringing him to Mullins Hill. It was a special honour to be trusted, and my ma gave me two bob to spend on sweets if we went on to Killiney village. Liam was delighted too, as it was his first venture into the big boys' world, and when he found out that his comic-swapping hero Massey was coming he was delighted, and a smile stuck to his little face until Ben asked him why he had a gimp and that confused him so the smile dissipated and his expression turned back to normal.

Massey led the way, his robust frame filling the road as we walked through Beechwood Lawns and up the lane.

'Did I ever tell yah bout de time I wus down in de jungle?'

Massey was trying to show off to Liam so Ben, using his practised exasperated tone, said, 'Yeah a million times – wer sick of it.'

Massey pretended he was hurt by Ben so he went quiet. We made our way up by Thomastown and then crossing Avondale Road. The little road to the Golf Club was quiet and I stopped to look at the old Beechfield Hotel – my aunt got married there – but it was empty now and had been closed for so long it was starting to look derelict. Neither Massey or Ben had any interest in it so Massey got bored and, still trying to show off, picked up some loose pebbles; he started to throw them at the overhead streetlamps, hitting a couple, but the stones were too light to cause damage.

'Why's he doin dat?' Liam asked. Then he added, 'He will break 'em … an de cops will be after us.'

Ben laughed, 'Nah, he won't break 'em, Liam … he culdn't break anythin …' Ben picked up a bigger stone and although it didn't smash the glass it made a terrible noise so we legged it, with Liam keeping up till we got to the gate leading to the path that ran adjacent to the golf course. The course was quiet as it was mid-week and there was no one around.

Noggiiners

'Lookin farward to a drink outta one of dose bottles on de way back …' Massey was pointing at the stacked crates of empty bottles from the Golf Club bar, and the ladies who worked there were generous to thirsty walkers so sometimes they allowed us use the outside tap in the yard by the kitchen, and when they opened the window I could hear the faint hum of a fan running in the background.

'Mousey Johnson's a mare up,' Massey said suddenly.

'He is far fuckin sure,' Ben said caustically.

'Wat's a mare up?' Liam asked.

'Yah don't know wat a mare up is?' Massey smiled at Ben, but Liam looked at me beseechingly.

'It's wen a fella mares it up to de golf early in de mornin soes he can get two bags to carry.'

'Wat's wrong wit dat?' Liam said and he sounded like he knew his business.

'Yeah,' Massey said, 'Mousey Johnston is gonna get 'is head kicked in … he is taken all der bags …'

'He is … sure nobody else runs up at seven o'clock … jasus it's still dark … Massey's right der gonna kick his head in … an yer man de caddy master is doin nuthin aither …' I never saw Ben look so serious.

'Shh, der he is,' I say and Massey as quick as you like goes, 'Jack de nigger from Ballybrack.'

'Shur up da fuck he'll hear yah,' Ben warns.

'Howya Jack,' Massey says like he has known Jack all his life.

Jack is sitting on an upturned concrete block, relaxing; he sits outside the caddy master's shack catching the sun. He is sallow with an Indian look; I don't like his eyes – they

28

are a deep brown and they dart from one of us to the other … he is suspicious of us and he doesn't make any allowance for Liam. The very one, Mousey Johnson, appears from the caddy shack sporting his usual silly grin; Mousey is fair-haired and very skinny, and mumbles something to Jack, who doesn't acknowledge him but it is obvious that they are friendly – Jack reaches into his trousers pocket and produces a fag, which he lights.

'Wer yah goin, Massey?' Mousey asks.

'You're Massey?' Jack says.

'Goin ta de village … we're gonna do de shop …'

Mousey was lost for words and Liam and I had made an effort to move on, but Ben was hanging on and said convincingly, 'Ta fuck we ar … yah still gettin up early, Mousey?'

Jack gave Ben a hollow look. ''Tis 'is own business,' Jack said.

Ben accepted it and started to follow us, but Massey lingered. 'How many bags can yah carry?'

Mousey, not wanting to divulge trade secrets, said, 'Mind yer nose.' Jack tipped the base of his own nose in support.

'Wus only askin.' Massey, getting the message, was coming after us.

'I hate mare ups,' he said, 'gives de udders fuck all chance.'

Liam stopped to look at this middle-aged man tee off … the tee was right by the entrance gate to the hill. The man was with his son and the teenager smiled over to acknowledge our respectful quietness.

'Shh,' Massey said unnecessarily … the middle-aged man smiled at us too as they set off even though he hadn't hit a good shot, and it was more than likely that his ball was lost in the boundary hedge.

'I like golf,' Liam announced but Massey ridiculed it, 'Fuckin poshies game.' Ben went to say something but then declined as we were on the path heading up the hill.

'Der was a plane crash,' I said specially for Liam's ears and he was all attentive – 'wher, wher' – down to our left was a deep chasm full of bulrushes surrounded by flat granite rocks. We never ventured down there but one of the flat granite rocks was stained by the constant dripping of dark water. In essence it looked like a huge oil stain and thus the plane crash.

'Wen wus it?' Massey asked, believing my story.

'Second World War.' I was convincing.

'Wher's de wreckage?' Liam asked intelligently.

'All gone be now,' Ben said in support of my tale.

'Wus der anywun killed?' Massey said, moving closer to inspect the dark-stained granite.

'All killed … the pilot an de co-pilot,' Ben said like there was nothing he didn't know.

'Very sad,' Liam said, wanting to move on like he didn't want anything to dampen his mood.

'Yahs ar havin us on.' Massey went to give Ben a friendly kick in the arse but Ben was too quick for him and Massey kicked the fresh air instead.

'Come on.' I started to trot. 'Let's climb de big rock.'

Liam started to trot too, just like he was on a horse, and all four of us measured, keeping to the mud track, jumping and avoiding invasive thorns and precocious nettles, we winding and twisting till we reached the small pond at the foot of the big rock. It was almost dried up but tiny pockets of water remained, guarded by loose stones.

'Hupe we find a frog.' Massey was excited.

'Ar der frogs?' Liam asked me. He was unsure who to believe anymore.

'Der is.'

Ben was on his knees searching the tall grass and the rushes, I was smelling that burnt smell of summer and the green smell of ferns …

'Shorty puts a straw up der arse and blows till dey explode,' Massey said it like he really needed to find a frog quick just to test the validity of Shorty's testimony.

'Nah, don't do dat.' Liam looked at me.

'Der's one,' Ben pounced, getting the knees of his jeans wet.

'Deadly,' Massey said, racing over to inspect the catch.

Ben held a tiny shivering frog in the fist of his left hand.

'Heold on till I geta straw,' Massey said and immediately started to search.

'Nah don't,' Liam said and I could see his eyes swell.

Ben opened his fist and the frog sat there for a few seconds. All our eyes were on Massey, who had found a suitable straw … 'Heold him,' he instructed but Ben made no effort and the frog leaped from his hand and disappeared into the grass.

'Wat da fuck?' Massey shouted, but Ben just laughed, 'I don't want bits a frog all over me.'

'It's cruel,' Liam said, and he put it right up to Massey who, looking down at him kindly, said, 'Sure I wus only messin … de tings yah learn down in de jungle.'

We climbed the big rock from the side, I giving Liam a

bunt and standing behind him should he slip and fall backwards. He was good though and once we reached the top he sat down and was safe.

The afternoon sun burned and soon I noticed Liam's legs go red so I told him to cover them with his jumper ... which he did and it was handy too as he could tie it around his waist when we moved on, so it would stop him from overheating. Massey was busy looking around him as Ben pointed out landmarks, and even though he should have known Massey sounded surprised that such things like Sallynoggin Church really existed. The distance brought with it a haze and the light flickered, and Massey was growing restless. Ben produced a bottle of Miranda orange that was full of Mi-Wadi – he had secreted it in the inside pocket of his jacket that trailed over his arm, he offered it round and though Massey thought about it he said no and only Liam took a slug. Ben took a good slug but there was still a half a bottle left when he put it away.

'I wanna make a fern camp ... who's up for it?' Massey was standing up and I was worried he was so close to the edge that he would slip and fall backwards, but he didn't, and soon we followed him deep into the jungle of ferns. We waded through and we got that sweet smell and Ben cursed when he put his hand accidently on slug spit. Massey was pulling at the stems, breaking some and bending others, and then he bashed the ferns back with his foot. Ben gave him a hand uprooting and tossing single ferns, then I imagined the ferns dying and screaming in their death as each feather weight sank amongst their compatriots.

'It's not big, it shuld be bigger,' Massey said, pulling more roots from the soft earth.

'It's huge,' a delighted Liam shouted; he was lifting and pulling like a good thing.

'Don't wanna too big,' Ben said solemnly before adding, 'keep it hidden from Bisto's camp.'

Bisto's camp was about twenty yards away, it was nothing really but a series of fine boulders resting on each other. Alongside there was a small grass area guarded by a six-foot ledge; the name Bisto was taken from the nick-name of an older neighbour, who took his handle from the gravy-making powder. How he got the name and how the camp came to be named in his honour nobody knew, but it was and that was all that we needed to know, and that it was a fact that Bisto was the oldest boy in the Durkan family, and he had found and named this place many years before we had ventured this way. Like all new and great things, we settled down within the confines of our fern camp. Liam thought it was something else; he tried lying on his back, his head propped by the wasted ferns, but then he turned on his side, facing one way, and then he tried the other.

Massey, after all the effort, was still looking bored and Ben was sitting upright, watching Massey. Ben amused himself taking out his bottle of Mi-Wadi, but he didn't drink any of it, he just played with it.

'Hey,' Ben said, 'Dah yah member Joe Durkan in "Who Falls de Best"?'

'Love dat,' Massey said, ready to talk over Ben.

'It wus de best fall ever,' I said.

'He belled it – culdn't believe it … he went flyin tru de sky like.'

Massey was on his feet – he threw his hands into the air to imitate a fella earth-bound.

'How he didn't break 'is snot,' Ben said.

'Wat happened to Joe?' Liam asked.

'He went flyin,' Massey said, 'right over Bisto's camp he took a bell.'

'He mus've fell twenty feet to de ferns below.' I smiled at Liam so he wouldn't be afraid.

'Gets up like nuthin happened, de mad yoke.' Ben stood up just because he was bored sitting down. 'Ar we goin over to de camp, lads?'

Ben started to kick something invisible in the ferns.

'Is dat a frog?' Massey wanted to know.

'It's jus Ben gone mad,' I said.

We were standing in the sea of ferns once more, moving very slowly till we met rising ground; Massey clamoured onto the edge of a huge rock, then he held his hand out for Liam, and then I bunted up and I was followed by Ben. The sun was still burning so I was glad that Liam had his jumper strapped around his waist. We stood on the ledge.

'Jump or lanch?' Massey asked.

'Yis can jump … me an Liam will lanch.'

'Alright,' Ben was gone, and he landed six feet below on his feet.

Massey, for all his bravado, hesitated and then Ben shouted at him, 'Jump you coward, an de child watchin yah!'

Massey jumped but he stumbled and cried out, 'Me fuckin foot!'

I lanched down, safely ensconced on the tight grass. Liam, brave as he was, lanched into my arms and I could feel his full weight as I set him to the ground.

We were exploring the large rocks; they had sudden holes within and some of them were tight and they dropped several feet. Massey was leading the expedition, followed by Ben and then me.

Liam slipped and then he somehow avoided falling into the one of the large holes, but in doing so he grazed his head off the underneath of the huge boulder.

'Jasus – shit – fuck!' I screamed as the blood poured from the side of Liam's head.

There was consternation and surprisingly it was Massey who was most upset: 'I shudda been behind 'im … poor fucker … dats a fuckin terrible gash … he'll want stitches.'

I wished that Massey would calm down as every time he mentioned stitches Liam started to sob.

Back on the muddy trail … the blood sticking to Liam's hair, I tried in vain to stem the flow with my hand … then Ben came up with an idea: 'I'll pour dis over it … stop de blood.'

I wasn't sure but I hadn't got a better idea so I agreed. Liam turned orange – the Mi-Wadi matted his hair

– and when I put my hand on him it stuck, and then I worried that I might infect the wound with my dirty hand. Massey, sensing my anxiety, said, 'He's quiet … hope he's no brain damage,' to which I retorted, 'Fuck off, Massey,' but Ben came in with, 'Aasy enough ta damage de brain.'

'We'll bring 'im home,' I said, taking charge.

Massey went red in the face and he went charging on ahead like he was some kind of hero leading us on through the jungle. Ben followed him but every now and then he stopped and looked back to check on me and Mi-Wadi-sticky Liam, who was now so quiet that I was really worried. When we passed the caddy master's shack there was no sign of Mousey or Jack, and the corrugated iron structure was locked. On the golf course an old man scuffed his shot down the fairway. It continued to bounce, running on forever towards the green, but in the end it just failed to make it. He came stomping down the fairway followed by his partner, a stout woman with a very serious face, and they checked us out as they went by, but they didn't say anything and neither did we.

'Frog,' Massey pounced.

He came out of the long grass with a sizable frog; the frog sat bemused on his hand.

'Any straws?' Massey said but then, seeing Liam's distress, he said, 'Nah worries we'll let yah go,' and Ben taking the frog put it down on the grass verge and the frog just stood there in no hurry like till he tapped his behind with the toe of his shoe, and frog leaped into the under-growth and safety.

'Wat if I've brain damage?' Liam asked suddenly as we

went through the swinging gate by the Golf Club.

'No way,' I said, putting a consoling arm around his shoulder.

'Nah,' Ben says, 'tell yah wat, sing a song, Liam; see if yah member de words … den we'll know.'

Liam slowed a little, 'Right,' he said, 'Where have you been all day, Henry, my son / Where have you been all day, my beloved one / Away on the meadow, away on the meadow, / Make my bed, I've a pain in my head / And I want to lie down.'

Massey, who was ten yards ahead, came running back. 'Luv dat song,' he joined in. Soon all four of us sang the only verse we knew … but we sang it all of the way down the golf road and across to Avondale and down the lanes till we reached the Noggin.

Ben's mother was standing at her front door and when she saw us lead little Liam up the garden path she wailed, as she mistook the Mi-Wadi stains for blood. There was no consoling her as she examined the gash on Liam's head. However, our luck was in, as Jackie Kingston, alighting from the bus, came over to investigate the consternation, and there was nothing for it but to bring Liam down to St Michael's for stitches, so off he went with Jackie on the same bus as she had just arrived on. She leading him by the hand like he was a tiny lamb; he waved at us as the bus powered past. Mrs Mooney had gone in for a cup of tea to settle her nerves and I was left so as to inform my mother of the tragedy when she returned from her errand.

'It mus be sore?'

'Wat?' Ben said, sitting down on his doorstep.

'Gettin a straw up de arse.' Massey said, 'I'm goin home far a piss.' He added as he walked towards the gate, 'Maybe a frog don't feel nuthin … I dunno.'

'Maybe,' I said.

'Nah, I'd say it hurts like mad,' Ben said.

Visits

1984

The rains had gone. Periodically buses slushed through the dark waters on the side of the road, dirty water waded over the pavement, making it dark brown – it was certain, though, that the drying wind would return all to white. Concepta walked slowly, feeling her knee was sore from the bang, the bottles in the shopping bag lethal bang bang against her right knee as she went through the gate.

She noticed the rain had combed the tip of the hedge in a thin film but she resisted the urge to wipe her hand across it. There was always something magical in the disturbance but only in the anticipation, somehow the results of same were never quite as interesting.

She fumbled the front door key and the hallway was dark, as only the low red light of the Sacred Heart lit the landing. Mother sat at the kitchen table – she was worried-looking but when she spoke she was surprisingly jovial.

'Johnny was always great with the sums – you wudn't remember; he knew all of his tables by the time he was seven.'

'Jesus I do, Mother, he used to drive me mad rhyming it off day after day.'

'Larry was more into fixing things.'

'Yeah – but Johnny always had that sumthin; yah know that's why he ended up rich.'

'Rich?'

'Yeah – well he's not short.'

'He has all of those children to mind ...'

'Pity Larry never had kids.'

'He didn't have time, Concepta – Larry didn't have enough time.'

'Do you think he will like the place?'

'He will, sure what's changed since Daddy died? Only the old hedges have gone wild 'cause I can't be standin on the chair to cut them.'

'Keep tellin yah we should get Ben Mooney to do it – give him a few bob; the young fella is well able – I was only sayin it to Joseph at the Bingo – "What's little Ben up to?" and Joseph says, "He's finished with school now and he's lookin for work."'

Concepta laid the shopping bag on the kitchen floor. Her Mother lifting her lower body from the chair; eyed it with anticipation and Concepta opened it wearily.

'I got the bottles of sherry; I love your trifle.'

'I have loads to ask Johnny – important things; like why he didn't come home for the funerals ... I missed him so much at Daddy's funeral. I was angry that he didn't make Larry's; you know how I feel about Johnny. I hate bein angry with him, Concepta.'

'I know, Mother – hang on I will make us a cuppa – Johnny told you that he cudn't get away on account of the child been so sick – he can come home now. Nicola is better thanks be to God.'

'Yes, thanks be to God for that.'

Concepta emptied the bag. She placed the more expensive bottle of sherry on the table beside her mother, putting the cheaper one at the other end of the table. She wanted to make a quip about which one they should use for the trifle, but gauging her mother's mood she didn't dare.

'Here, I'll get you the photographs,' she said as a compromise; emptying the bag completely with a bag of broken biscuits and a box of Lyons Tea, along with some wrapped sausages and rashers. The photographs were held neatly behind the brass candlestick on the mantelpiece.

'Concepta, she's a sweetheart – look at her and her hair is growing again; what do you think of Johnny?'

'He's himself … he's getting balder.'

'Like his father.'

'Daddy wasn't that baldy, Mother – he still had some at the sides.'

'He was bald as a coot.'

'Never – Daddy was never as bald as Johnny …'

'It's a sign of brains … so they say!'

'Do they?'

'It's a known fact – bald men are brainier than men with hair …'

'Never!'

''Tis true, Concepta.'

'Sure Breen the butcher is bald and he is a thick – here I will pour the tea …'

'Maybe not in every case, Concepta, it's the rule of thumb in general like … lovely cup of tea ah look at this one of the whole family – my God, Sinéad has gone a size and Matthew too – Jesus he is taller than his father?'

'It's Brian I feel sorry for – his poor burnt face – imagine been scalded by a hot kettle and he only five years old?'

'Johnny says he's getting on with it, he's a feisty chap by all accounts …'

There was a silence whilst they countenanced the gravity of poor Brian's burns.

'Are you sorry you never went?'

'Yer daddy wudn't travel – he didn't like leavin home; he used to say, let the children come see us – he always added, sure haven't we a grand place!'

'Save for me, Mother, there was no getting rid of me.'

'They say only the blessed stay with their parents all of their lives …'

'Nah, they don't, Mother, yer just makin that up.'

Concepta got up, pretending to fix the drying cloth – it was a good excuse, hanging untidily from the backdoor – she straightened it, noting that it was badly stained down one side, needed a wash. Through the glass in the kitchen door she saw the wet afternoon: the rain had darkened the gable walls of the houses out the back and all was quiet, not a sinner moved, and the wet air clung onto the world like a terrified child.

'How do you think she looks?'

'She's fatter, Mother – maybe a bit narkier lookin.'

'He could have done so much better than her, you know?'

'I know.'

'He could have married Annie Dwane – you know her father was a bookmaker – and her brother took it over. She was from the right side of the tracks, too – a gorgeous Dalkey woman nah Johnny slipped up there. I can never understand it; they were as thick as thieves; then he just suddenly abandons her to go to England with yer wan.'

'Maybe he had to?'

'What you mean, Concepta?'

'Nuthin, Mother; I just mean that maybe he had no choice like?'

'There are always choices – he just made the wrong one, that's all.'

'Whatever you say.'

'Men are like that, impetuous. They're ruled by other things – common sense never comes into it.'

Concepta went to sit back down, sadly; there only so much fiddling one could do with a drying cloth. She thought of mentioning her knee but she chose not to – her mother was reminiscing and was best left. She dragged her chair across the lino; Concepta hated the feel of it; it was cold and dirty on the kitchen floor.

'Was Daddy like that … Do you want more tea?'

'No – he wasn't, yer father wasn't like other men; he wasn't like that – if I drink any more tea, Concepta, I will burst – no, I am fine for all.'

'I am makin another cup for myself, I was thinkin if it stops raining I'm going to dig that patch over by Mooney's railings – I want to plant some lettuce.'

'Lettuce – sure the summer is on the wane; the frost will kill it. Jesus will you make sure not to dig up old Blackie?'

'Blackie's buried by the Cassidys, I'll be miles away.'

'Pity yah wudn't get out a chair and cut the hedge?'

'Yah, I know, I wud but I might get one of my dizzy spells and fall over; then what?'

'Then I can ask Ben Mooney to do it.'

'Yer impossible, Mother … How many years since we buried Blackie?'

'He died the year before yer daddy – so it's five years now.'

'I never seen Larry cry as a man – but Jesus he cried for that dog.'

'The dog was his life – followed him everywhere. We should have called him "Shadow", the big black mutt.'

'Yah Shadow wud have been a perfect name.'

'Shadow Kelly.'

'The kids comin in and puttin dandelions and daises on his grave.'

'Not many kids here now – those kids are all teenagers. It would kill them to say "hello" to yah.'

'Ah that tea is too weak, Mother. I'll give it a stir – the kids don't like us over the ball and the flowers – they wanted to kick ball but daddy wanted to grow flowers.'

'He was entitled to grow his flowers.'

'I know – but taken in the ball drove the kids' bananas. I used to say to 'im, "Throw it back out," but yah know when he was stubborn and if I said anythin he wud do the opposite.'

'He always threw it back in the end, Concepta, like he never burst it – he watched them playin when he was cuttin the hedge; he'd tell me that Massey was brutal, but Seanie Cassidy and Ben Mooney were footballers.'

Her mother took to playing with her empty cup. This was something she did when she was either tired or bored; then, noticing that Concepta was looking at her, she stopped for a second, only resuming when Concepta started to speak once more.

'Larry cud play but Johnny cudn't kick the ball.'

'That's because Johnny had the jaundice so he had no energy to go play with the others – anyways Larry was always out; but Johnny loved his comics … football wasn't for him; he was never goin to make a George Best.'

'Georgie is the very best … Johnny didn't even follow the football, Mother … funny he never took to it but Larry was mad into it – two brothers so different, do yah think Larry and Johnny got on at all?'

'How do yah mean?'

'Like they were never close like.'

'That's because Johnny was twelve years older ... sure Larry could nearly have been his son; Johnny was a man through most of Larry's childhood ... they didn't not get on.'

'Larry never went over to see him.'

'Ah, Concepta, he was busy with the garage and Joan was trying for the babies ... maybe it wasn't Johnny, maybe it was Rita he didn't like ... she was always very cold towards him if I remember ...'

'She hated me – I pleaded with her to be somethin at the wedding, even a flower girl wud have done.'

'I know, she would begrudge you a sausage, that one ... She had it all packed with her own crowd. I was ragin that Larry wasn't the best man; imagine Michael Kearns, like; who ever saw Michael Kearns before or after the wedding, he just sprang up out of nowhere.'

'Mick Kearns was a friend of her brother's, wasn't Johnny terribly foolish to agree to it, though; like he didn't stand up for his own, that's for sure ... You wud have thought he might stand up for his own.'

'The whole thing was wrong, Concepta – why he didn't stick with Annie Dwane I will never know; all wud have been so different.'

*

'There he is, it's Johnny, look its Johnny – that's him alright, that's Johnny.'

'Let me see ... it's him, Mother, who is that with him?'

'It's her. God, Concepta, he brought her.'

'No.'

'There not unloading cases, are they?'

'I can't see with the hedge.'

'I didn't know she was comin. Jesus the room isn't ready ... not for her.'

'Hold on, Mother, he just has a bag over his shoulder; der's no cases.'

'Thanks be to God – go and open the door; is me hair alright?'

'You look great, relax, you'll have a heart attack.'

The sun came alive across the garden, its soft heat reviving the dark dead circles of plants. Johnny walked through the gate with his chest bursting through his shirt; he looked fresh, wearing an ordinary sports jacket and thin slacks. She followed in military fashion, staying bang in line with the vagrant wisp of hair jangling from the top of his head. She was pert and serious and her hair was tightly bundled; she was elegant but without the fuss; she lived in shadows under a plain white hat with a short brim. He walked quickly and she stayed behind him, moving in unison, matching his fits and starts.

'Hello, Johnny.'

'Mother.'

'You look smashin!'

'Can I use the toilet, Mrs Kelly? I'm bursting.'

'Of course, Rita; Concepta will show you.'

'It's ok; I think I remember.'

'How was the trip?'

'Hi yah, Concepta – you're looking well.'

'Try my best, Brother – but it's hard to keep up with the likes of you.'

'Did you bring the car?'

'I did, Mother – we were going to hire one but you know that works out very expensive, so we brought the oul wreck over. We chugged our way up the oul Noggin Hill.'

'Come on in, son – we'll put on a fry – Concepta will get it on – she still gets the deals from Joe Breen.'

'He's still alive? Blimey, I thought he'd have retired by now – but sure he probably isn't that old, is he?'

'What age is he, Concepta? Tell Johnny how old he is.'

'Breen is seventy just last week – he was goin on about his sisters throwin a party for 'im; will Rita go a few of Breen's sausages?'

'She will eat the leg off the chair – we're ravenous, we didn't eat on the boat – it was choppy, you know? I said to Rita, don't bother to eat 'cause we will just end up throwin it all up so we will – she was mad with me, but we didn't puke either.'

'I would love two sausages,' Rita said, returning from the loo, 'whatever else, maybe an egg – do you have pudding? In England we can't get decent puddin – it's a shame, isn't it, Johnny?'

'The English don't get the Irish traditions, do they?'

'I got puddin even though Mother hates it – I love it – we have rashers and eggs and some lovely fresh bread in for yis.'

'Great, I am dyin for puddin,' Rita said, going over to the counter to examine the raw pork.

'Spot on, Sis ... so how's my oul mum, hey?'

'I'm strugglin without you, Johnny – pity you couldn't make the funerals, we really missed you – I wanted to tell ...'

'Oh no, Mother ...'

'Mrs Kelly, please don't cry.'

'Ah, Mother.'

'No, Rita dear, you have no idea how much we missed Johnny; first his poor old father and then Larry all in a space of a few years ... it was awful.'

'Bloody awful, Johnny ... Rita, I'll stick you on an extra rasher ...'

'Larry was missing you, too – and then he and Joan broke up and he came back here to live, and then he got sick. It all happened so fast ...'

'Hey, Mum, I'm here now – so all is ok; fret no more, Johnny's home, hey?'

An uneasy silence fell. Johnny was trying to overcome the sadness with his natural exuberance and inexplicably he started to rub his hands feverously. Rita just sat looking uncomfortable – this was what she had expected, she had even prepared for; it just was that she didn't expect it all to be so intense.

'Thanks, Johnny, you're a great son. I could hug you to death ... thanks for all you did and thanks for the money ...'

'What money?'

'The money towards the funerals, Rita, what else?'

'We had to pay for Nicola's treatment in America; we had poor Brian's accident; we didn't have any money to give away, did we, Johnny?'

'Well I had to dig it up, didn't I – I had an old endowment

policy; sure we'll not chat about all that now – we are only
in the door and the grub is smellin great.'

'But we needed the money for Nicola.'

'And we got it my love.'

'Only through the good will of the people of the parish
– we were well short Johnny.'

'I don't get this, Rita.'

'We hadn't enough to pay for our daughter's treatment
but you sent money back here to help pay for funerals; get
that.'

'Sit down, Rita, ok, we were a bit strapped.'

'A bit – we were thousands short.'

'Sit down – sure didn't we manage in the end, all's well
that ends well, hey?'

'I won't sit down at this table with you people who've
stolen the funds we needed to save our Nicola; for what
your belligerent father and yer halfwit brother …'

'Oh my God.'

'Settle, Mother – who are you to come into our home
with my brother; cause consternation as soon as you hit the
kitchen – like who are you? We sat up nights here worried
about little Nicola, worryin about you and Johnny as well
… The cheek: my mother never asked Johnny for a shilling
– but you come in here judging us; what an insult, missus,
whatever Johnny gave her was out of the goodness of his
heart … my mother minded him for all those years; me
father watched over him too – you wud begrudge him that,
and to pay his respects to his only brother …'

'Yeah, well, he never had a decent word to say about
either of them – accordin to Johnny your father was a

tyrant and yer brother was lazy and slow ...'

Concepta went to console her mother, whose hands covered her eyes, meanwhile Rita was stomping her right shoe against the lino just like a bull. Johnny succumbed and all the colour drained from his face before he spoke.

'Stop it now, all of you, come on. I haven't stepped in here for twenty years an already the house is shaken with the sound of your cantankerous voices – yes, Rita, I cashed in the ould endowment policy, but at that stage the fund-raising was providin what Nicola needed – the news was good in general; the doctors were positive ... I just wanted to give my little ould mum a hand, was that so bad? My father was a tyrant, indeed I loved him just the same and as for Larry, he was the apple of my eye – yeah, he could be a handful and he had some funny ways – but I loved him just the same. When he died I cried for three days an you know that, Rita, 'cause you listened to me cry – and never once did you come near me to show me even an ounce of comfort ... but hell let's not dwell, we will rise again ... come let's eat breakfast, please, all, in honour of my father and my kid brother, let's sit and eat.'

*

'She is gone to show him where she buried Blackie.'

'I'm sorry for my outburst, Mrs Kelly – we've been under terrible stress these last years, with Nicola and Brian. Johnny's business hasn't been good, the demand for electrical goods has fallen; to be honest we can't compete with the big boys anymore – they wiped us out.'

'Sorry to hear that, Rita ... do you want more tea?'

'No, thanks.'

'You must have been ravenous.'

'We were; it's a long journey – you know Johnny hasn't been well these last few years? He's developed a heart condition – nothing too serious but he has been warned to slow down ... I thought it might help him to come home and see you and Concepta – visit the graves, you know, finally pay his respects. I suppose I am a hard woman, Mrs Kelly, I can't empathise with people enough, but it's a fault I always had, even when I was young; it's ridiculous but to be honest my own mother was worse!'

'We all have our crosses, Rita; Johnny he never mentioned his heart in any of his letters.'

'He didn't want to worry you.'

'He looks so good, hold on I think they're coming back in, poor Johnny, am I to lose him too?'

'No, I hope not ... look, he's so embarrassed, Mrs Kelly, but you see we're broke – we had to sell the business and we got nought for it. The younger ones are still at school so we need a place to live just temporary till we get back on our feet – it would allow us sell the house, you know – just Johnny and me and Nicola and Brian ... what do you think?'

'I dunno, I mean I'd love to have you both but it just seems like a drastic move. Are you sure you have to do this, like, coming back to Ireland and upsettin the kids? Then there's Concepta; she's very delicate, you know, and she is used to it just been ourselves.'

'I can ask my sister, Mrs Kelly, but whatever happens we have to come home – we have no choice.'

She watched Johnny looking all out of place; he looked older now as he traipsed across the mud. Concepta walked after him, smiling, it was lovely to see but the memory was from way back in their childhood, and she knew that she had seen a similar image before but it was from so long ago, and now it hurt her to try and remember it.

'The old dog found a good resting place – bet you miss him, Mum?'

'Ah, Johnny, he was a great old friend – he was Larry's dog, really, but sure we all loved him.'

'We were going to get a dog for Brian so we picked up this Boxer bitch, take the bloody hand off yah – so we gave up on it in the end, stupid dog.'

'Brian had been through enough – we didn't want his face bitten off as well as burnt – I don't like dogs, Mrs Kelly.'

'Sure there's nothing wrong with that … each to their own, Rita. Are you going to rest before going to the grave-yard? Yah know it was nice that we could put Larry in with daddy; Joan was very agreeable about it I have to say.'

'Was she? I tell you, Mum, she wasn't the worst; I did tell you, didn't I?'

'You always said that, Johnny.'

'We could do with an hour or two, Mrs Kelly … How about we go this afternoon, all of us? There's loads of room in the car; sure we are only going as far as the Deansgrange.'

'I'm up for that, Mother, we better let these two rest, and by the time I tidy up …'

'Whatever you say, Concepta.'

Blood

1983

Larkin didn't always take to Murray, yet Murray had a soft spot for Larkin and for Dunne. Larkin liked Dunne but just not as a friend, he liked him because Dunne was somebody to look up to, and particularly because Dunne bullied Murray and humiliated him at every opportunity. Murray took it well, sometimes his bottom lip quivered and his voice got all high-pitched, but he never really retaliated or put it up to Dunne. Occasionally Dunne would slap him on the back, acting like he was his best pal. Murray loved this; he would break out in a grin that conquered his whole face. Dunne most likely wanted him to go and get more pints, and most times Murray got up and went gladly – it was like he had no idea that Dunne was just using him.

Larkin liked the Graduate in the afternoon and he didn't mind the early evening either but he didn't like the nights at all. The afternoons were for serious drinkers, people in search of conversation. They didn't mind who it was with either as they could talk to a fella three stools down or shout at the old man sitting over by the toilet; some just wanted a word with the friendly barman, but others were full-time professional drinkers, who sat removed from the company, ordering chasers with their pints – they were palliative, forever silent, only to shrug should anyone ask them a question.

Larkin preferred the quiet ones, the fellas that barely nodded when they were leaving with dignity, walking by with a rolled-up newspaper under their armpit; always looking solitary and very intelligent, significantly if any of them gave him recognition he was delighted as, paradoxically, these were the guys he looked up to. They were proper drinkers, the pioneers of alcoholism, the cagy loners driven to the bar by life experience, by nagging wives, or maybe both. He didn't like the new trend where these lushes were allowed join in, starting with one or two they arrived in out of the blue and they mostly hung in with the better-off crowd who congregated down the bar; these women stood chatting gaily with gin and tonics or cocktails in their hands. Murray said something about their tight behinds and in response Dunne threw his eyes to Heaven and smirked at Larkin.

'They're well past it,' Dunne said.

'Nah, yer one blondie isn't bad.' Murray deliberately stared at Blondie till she became conscious of him; she was exasperated and she turned the other way soes he could only see her side on. Nervously she whispered something to her companion, Big Frank, who was a studious fella with black-framed glasses; stealthily he peered around her, eyeing Murray, who somehow found the manners to look away.

'Jasus Murray, Big Frank will kill yah, don't be fooled by 'im, he wud fuckin kill yah, wudn't he, Dunner?'

Larkin gazed at Dunne, and Dunne, rising to it, said, 'He wud – the Gum Man lit his newspaper and he went ballistic – tell yah, Murray, he decked the Gum Man, put him out like.'

'He lit his paper?'

'Yeah,' says Dunne, 'he asked him to look up the time of a race at Leopardstown, an wen Frankie opened up his paper the Gum Man lit it; the fuckin ting went up in flames an Frankie still holdin it!'

'Jasus,' Murray said, making sure to not to look in Big Frank's direction.

'An he laid him out?'

'He did – amazed yah never heard of dat, how dah ya tink the Gum Man got the shiner on his face?'

'He told me he fell against his doorstep wen he wus locked.'

'Didn't want yah to know so,' Larkin advised.

Murray went quiet – he was insulted as in truth he always regarded the Gum Man as a real friend who told him everything – annoying not to tell him something like this, amounted to a betrayal, inevitably both Larkin and Dunne knew this.

Dunne said innocently, 'Surprised he didn't tell yah, Murray, he told everyone else, pints so?' Murray stared at him like it wasn't his round as he got the last. 'Here,' Dunne said smartly, 'go get 'em.' He hands him some money, 'Keep the change, an keep yer eyes to yourself, we don't want Big Frank down on us.'

Murray took the money and walked lazily to the bar; Big Frank ignored him, however, he kindly placed his hand on Blondie's shoulder. Larkin couldn't help but look over at her: she was weather-beaten, dreadfully used-looking and her pale skin was basted with some kind of white powder, all the same it still let the imperfections through.

'She does've a nice arse,' Dunne laughed.

'But she's rough,' Larkin replied, 'an yer man will burst the Gum Man for not tellin him about Big Frank's punch.'

'He will, an de Gum Man won't know wat the fuck he is on about!'

'He won't,' Larkin said.

Larkin was thinking about the furnace, the molten aluminium with the ladle pouring this liquid metal slowly into the moulds. Taylor said he was no good at it. Taylor didn't say it to him, he said it to Murray and then Murray told Larkin. After a few goes the ladle got heavy and the tiny moulds shrank. Larkin found the handles of the mould stiff and he knew that Taylor was watching his every move. Larkin knew about Taylor from the bar – he was mostly a late-night drinker but when he was on shifts he could turn up during the day. It was amazing how Taylor changed – invariably he was all happy-go-lucky in the bar, a gas man, yet in the heat of the foundry he was a dictator and a bully.

Taylor got him taken off the moulds – that was the first thing he did, banishing him to the saw outside the foundry. The second thing he did was have Larkin removed from the foundry shifts altogether and Larkin was wary of him after that; in the end it was because of Taylor and his bullying that Larkin ended up punching holes in metal all day long, endless days standing still till eventually his back was ready to cave in and his head was ready to melt. The Gum Man said that Taylor was a renowned wife-beater, a true house-devil rumour had it that he was ridin some oul wan from Shankill for years.

Larkin believed the Gum Man mainly because he wanted to, but the Gum Man was prone to exaggeration; he was a renowned storyteller and he told lots of stories, but most of them were not true. This time Larkin was about to forgo logic, and if the Gum Man said all that about Taylor, well, it just had to be true.

Larkin figured Taylor to be a Mexican as he strolled in looking different out of his blue work coat. He was portly in his civvies and he arrived full of smiles behind Murray's curly head.

'Straight to the pub to spend yer money, Murray, an you,' he looked at Larkin, 'are you not on today?' He is only short of wearing a sombrero. Suddenly there was a high whistling sound and Larkin had Clint Eastwood music playing in his head.

'Me oul wan's sick.' It was half true.

'Wat yah doin in here so?'

'Havin a pint,' Larkin said cheekily.

'I didn't see yah so.' Taylor, laughing like a bandito, walked over to the bar where he had some trouble picking a stool but eventually he chose one with a back on it.

He was big on the stool and his arse was too big for the hole in the wood. Taylor rested his arms giant-like on the counter; shockingly, Larkin noticed that Taylor's dark hair was matted to his head with hair oil, then for a minute he even thought it was a rug. Larkin wasn't lying about his oul wan – her cough was much worse, sometimes she was having trouble breathing – he was planning to go home early and make her tea. Would Taylor rat on him? He wasn't so sure as he might have had a reputation for being a ballox, yet Larkin never took him for a rat, still Taylor was a company man true and true.

'He won't say nuthin,' Murray piped up as if he was reading Larkin's mind.

'Be hated if he rats on yah!'

'Yeah well,' Larkin sighed, 'der's nuthin I can do about it anyways.'

'Murray, go get three pints will yah like a good lad!'

Murray shook his head. 'I'm not goin up to stand beside him – I see enough of Taylor at work – he annoys de heart out of me.'

'Well who should go up den? Larkin's shit scared of him.'

'I am not.'

'Yes yah are,' Murray laughed.

'I am da fuck,' Larkin said seriously.

'I'd go meself but me leg,' Dunne joked.

'Yeah why don't you go yerself?' Murray pleaded.

Blood

'Someone go,' Larkin said, looking over at Taylor. Big Frank nodded over at Taylor but the suspicious Blondie chose to ignore him and in fairness Taylor was drinking his stout; he had no interest in Blondie.

'How's it hangin?' Big Frank shouted across. Taylor was drinking more of his pint, but when he put it down he went, 'I'm still stoking the fires, Frank.'

'Are you finished with the car business then?' Frank shouted over, 'Dis years.'

Taylor gave his Mexican smile: he was pleased that Frank recognised him and was wondering about the car business, 'Got out of it years ago – I'm makin money now, stokin the fires in the foundry down in Pottery Road.'

'In Mcalpines?'

Taylor just smiled and Frank asked, 'Are they British?'

'No. Yanks,' Taylor enlightened him.

'The Yanks are good employers – better than the Brits, I always said that.' Big Frank was distracted by Blondie – she was pointing at a painting on the wall. It was a print of a vase full of flowers and Big Frank gladly reengaged with her. Taylor was waiting for him to turn around but he didn't, so after a while he just returned to staring into his pint.

Larkin threw his money onto the table. 'You go up, Murray, you fat head.'

'Nah, it's not my turn.'

'No messin,' Dunne turned to Murray, 'if I go up he will start on at me about de fuckin scratcher. I will end up thumpin 'im.' Murray stood up; taking Larkin's money, he strode up to the bar. Taylor saw him coming and his face lit up. Larkin wondered how he did it, sometimes his face was pale and then he would go red, and then other times he looked sallow under a different light.

The Gum Man came in and Larkin wondered why pork butchers looked like pigs. The Gum Man had a big round face with wide shoulders; inexplicably the rest of him was in good shape but some people thought he was too thin. The Gum Man was afflicted with a stutter, especially when he was nervous. He stopped in his tracks when he eyed Taylor.

'Eh puuuut oooone onnnn for mee.'

Murray just laughed and he ordered another stout.

The Gum Man sat between Larkin and Dunne, keeping his back to Taylor.

'Issss heee look inn ooover?'

'Fuck 'im,' Dunne said.

'Hes chattin to Murray.' Larkin suddenly realised the Gum Man theory; besides looking like a pig, he had no front teeth and even without his stutter words would have had great difficulty forming.

'Heee's aa cunnnt.' The Gum Man eyed his fresh creamy pint, he moved it from the bare table to the protection of a beer mat. Dunne watched him do it, fascinated that it didn't spill.

'Weee had a hard dayyy of it.' The Gum Man was relaxing.

'IIIII wasssss witttt Peeter Boyyle – down in the Viccctor Hotel.'

Dunne did his usual, throwing his eyes to Heaven, they disappearing for a split second under his eyelids. Murray was back sitting down and Larkin eyed him, sure that he was trying to eye up Blondie again.

'Peeter Boyyle is sum mann to kill piggss – he killed threeee of 'em dids morninnn – der was blooooood all over theeee place.'

'Didn't know he killed his own pigs – wher, in Cabinteely or in de Noggin?' Dunne asked.

'Dooown in de Noggin!' the Gum Man said with some satisfaction. 'I cleaned up de blooood – fuckin smell was cattt.'

'Big Frank is lookin over.' Murray said, 'Sooo,' the Gum Man was looking at him, 'so yah never told me about the fuckin newspaper; you settin Big Frank on fire.'

'Waaat?'

'Heard he gave yah a right box,' Murray said.

Dunne kicked the Gum Man under the table and Larkin winked at him.

'Big FFFrankk …' The Gum Man wasn't catching on. He looked around. Big Frank was staring down but he was really giving Murray a dirty look.

'Data wat yah get for settin fire to 'is paper,' Murray taunted.

'Waaat?' the Gum Man was mystified.

'Did we have a bet on United?' Taylor stood big over the table, and it was obvious he was on his way out as there was no pint resting on the bar.

'Jasus I caaaaan't re ree re remember?'

'Yah can't remember?' Taylor was smiling but it masked a much deeper seriousness.

'I met yah down in Baker's one night about a month ago – I took United and you took Liverpool, isn't that right?'

'Hhhhoww muuuch?'

'I shud tell yah fifty, we only had a twenty spot – an I won of course.'

'I cccann't rememmmberr but I will take yer word.'

The gum man took a crumpled twenty from his wallet and handed it over. Taylor took it, his whole head smiling now. 'Nice one,' he said and left.

'Cuuuntt – I was fuckin locked dat nighttt.'

'Toe rag,' Larkin said.

'How many pigs wud Peter Boyle kill in a week?' Dunne asked.

'Depends ooon theee week!' the Gum Man said.

'Give me an average?' Dunne persisted.

'Threeee aaa day, moost weeks,' the Gum Man swallowed his pint; he was still smarting over the twenty.

'Big Frank is still lookin at yah,' Murray said. 'Don't know why yah never told me he decked yah; were yah embarrassed or wat?'

The Gum Man had given up on Murray so he went, 'I hearrr MMary Warn err is gone from the VVictor!'

It didn't register with Murray and Dunne was thinking of another pint but Larkin said, 'Where is she gone?'

'Shee's gonne hom eee I tinkk.'

The Gum Man bought a round – somehow time raced away, and then it was time to go home as night approached and the next drinking shift was due in.

The Gum Man had a car and he gave Murray a lift. Dunne and Larkin walked through Killiney shopping centre, taking the shortcut through Beechwood Lawns on to Rochestown Park. Dunne got off here and Larkin walked on alone. He was thinkin of Mary Warner; the Gum Man said she had gone home but he wasn't sure, where was home? She came from some small village in Kildare; she had come to the Victor Hotel to work as a chambermaid, making beds and cleaning rooms, it was a job but it beat pouring liquid aluminium into moulds or pressing holes in metal.

Mary was a strong-looking, robust character – she was sure of herself and she liked to flirt with men. Larkin feared her: she made him nervous and when he went to the Victor for a pint he was awkward if he met her, sometimes she came into the bar to chat with the fellas but he always stayed quiet. But he loved her face; her skin was firm and smooth but more importantly she had delicious eyes that screamed at you if you met them full on. Mary wore lots of mascara – it somehow remained steadfast on her eyelashes – and he loved her hair, she had it long and straight and it could be dark or it might be fairer depending on her mood. The rumours were that if she had drink taken she might take you around the back of the hotel and give you a ride. Larkin visualised her as he went turning right just before the cul de sac, he was nearly home.

One night he was smuggled into the garden ballroom; it was a member of staff's engagement party.

It was his night as Mary set on him after he had spoken

a few words to her at the bar. When the music was over he slipped outside with her and she brought him down the garden, stopping under a clump of trees. She kissed him wildly, biting into his neck. Maybe it was the drink, he didn't really know, but he took control and he slipped his hand under her dress.

'Don't,' she said. 'Like I want to – but I am havin me period.'

'Oh – dat's alright.'

'You wouldn't mind the blood.'

'No.'

'It's not nice, like?'

She slipped off her pants and she allowed him mount her. It didn't last long as she kissed him and gave him her tongue and he finished, and when he withdrew a security light from the hotel illuminated all and he was disgusted at the treacle-like blood that dripped down his thighs, staining his trousers and underpants.

'Not nice, is it?' she said.

Larkin was home; he was disturbed the hall light wasn't on but his oul wan always left it on.

In the hall he reached for the light switch. He was thinking of the Gum Man and the killing of pigs, with blood everywhere and in his head he was hearing the relentless screaming of pigs.

The oul wan was lying face down by the living room door, blood flowing from her mouth. Larkin ran to her lifeless body and this fatty blood deep red saturated her tender pale skin.

Hate Lessons

1978–1985

The first time he brought her to the house she felt comfortable. His mother was there; she had a nice smile. She was just sixty years old then but she looked older, though mainly because she had heavy lines on her forehead and she was exceptionally thin. Mrs Tynan's smile was genuine if a bit reticent, yet Grace mused that it must have been awkward for her as well. The house was as Philip described: a Corporation house built to standard – it had a nice-sized front garden with no flowers or ornamental add-ons, and because there was no front hedge all was bare by the railings. The back garden was longer; it was shaped in a triangle before getting dark where it narrowed to where a clump of nettles had grown so tall, and there was a stone shed to the left. The door was padlocked and Grace knew by the look of it that it hadn't been opened for some time.

Mrs Tynan offered her tea. 'Philip won't drink coffee, so tea is all we have.'

She went to the sink by the window and put the kettle on.

'Lousy weather – you wouldn't know what it's gonna do – not like July!'

'No – it's been lousy.' Grace smiled at Philip, who was wiping his glasses.

'Weather is weather,' he said. 'What is it with women and weather?'

'We like it to be nice,' Grace said softly.

Mrs Tynan was reaching to the cupboard to get a plate to put the biscuits on and the kettle was steaming and bubbling, ready to switch off. Grace kicked Philip under the table in an effort to distract him from his glasses and get him to pay attention.

'You have your house lovely, Mrs Tynan.'

'Oh I dunno, it's a mess – you'd best call me Maura – if you're going to live here after the wedding you can't very well be calling me Mrs Tynan, can you?' She brought the plate of biscuits to the table and then she went and took three mugs from the hooks under the dresser. She was humming to herself as she poured milk from a bottle into a china jug, determined; she was still humming when she placed the jug on the table.

'Will I pour the tea?' Grace asked.

'Nay you won't, girl, you are a guest in my kitchen.'

For a moment Grace didn't know if she had offended her as Mrs Tynan went quiet as she poured the tea into the mugs, laboriously carrying each mug steadily to the table.

Finally, she sat down and beamed. 'So we get a trip to Athlone, do we?' and before Grace could answer she went on, 'You know Athlone is a long way from my home place in Donegal, I suppose most places are, but it's not so far from Sallynoggin, is it?'

'Bridget is driving you, Mother – we have it all organised – you can go down with Bridget and Marie and all of the gang; they're bringing two cars.'

'They're all driving, then – well, that's nice, and I hear we're staying in the Prince of Wales?'

'I told you all of this,' Philip said impatiently.

'Awk, I know, dear, but I love to hear these things over an over, now please indulge your poor mother.'

Mrs Tynan drank her tea gently, just like a lady. Grace stayed quiet for a moment, thinking of what to say next; self-consciously she didn't want to appear rude by hogging the conversation but finally the excitement won out.

'I've chosen the bridesmaids.' Grace waited for a reaction, but Mrs Tynan just looked at her blankly.

'My sister Helen and Teresa Fay, she was my best friend in school – we are neighbours like.'

'So who is best man, Philip?'

He was startled by the question; having lived away for so long it wasn't something he had paid much attention to. He had hemmed and hawed but he'd never reached a definitive decision, despite plenty of nagging from Grace.

'He hasn't decided yet,' Grace rushed to his defence.

'What?'

'I can't ask Barney; I haven't seen him for two years.'

'Barney.'

'Barney might turn up stewed,' Mrs Tynan said caustically.

Grace looked at Philip sternly but he just drank more of his tea, 'Barney's off the drink, he's back playin with the lads, ah Barney would be grand, but I was thinkin of Brian down in Athlone, he's been my mate for two years now.'

'Barney over my dead body, sure his mother would know all of our business, I don't care if they live next door but my business stays within this house – tell me who this Brian is?'

Grace noticed Mrs Tynan's anger and she wanted to scream stop, but just as quick she wanted to reach out and stroke her arm, but she didn't.

Brian was the best man. He was a small, ineffectual chap but he was a good footballer and he and Philip played for the factory team. Philip was transferred from the company headquarters in Dun Laoghaire; he hadn't got a great job but it was good enough working in the accounts department and he was really sharp with figures. One night Grace met him down the town in a bar – Philip was sitting in the corner on his own and she just happened to plonk herself down beside him. She was going on a hen's night out; as usual they had just stopped for a few warm-up drinks. He was so intense-looking and she noticing that he moved up a seat to allow the girls room.

'What's a fella like you doin on his own?' Grace asked.

Philip's forehead went red but his smile broke his embarrassment.

'Hopin to meet someone like you!'

All the girls went wooh – and one said, 'Cheeky.'

Philip reached for his pint needing, security.

'We're goin to a hen's – so don't mind us, some of these wanna get drunk before the party starts – are you from the town, I never see you around?' The girls had lost interest and were now chatting amongst themselves.

'I'm from Dublin, I'm workin here this last year and a half but I dunno it looks like I might be headin home soon – business isn't great, there's talk of cutbacks – we will see – I like this town.'

'I'm Athlone born and bred.'

'I'm from the Noggin!'

'The Noggin – where the hell is that?'

'Near Dun Laoghaire – we're a big Corporation estate – not like the little ones you have around here.'

'Our house is owned by the Council – me da pays rent, same thing.'

'What do you work at?'

'I work in Miller's, the drapery end.'

'Very nice.'

'And you?'

'Nielsen's.'

'They're big.'

'Not anymore,' Philip said ruefully.

The girls wanted to move on; gleefully, they started teasing Grace about Philip, saying things like, 'Leave him alone, the poor fella; you can't bring him tonight.' Philip just laughed but Grace let them go out the door. She was on her feet. 'I sometimes come in here on Wednesday nights – like if you're doin nothin – I sit over there at the end of the bar – I usually come with my friend Teresa but she's away in Majorca with her sister – might see you on Wednesday then?'

Philip smiled; it was the smile of a fellow who couldn't believe his luck. 'What time?' he said.

'About nine,' she shouted back and went chasing after her friends.

They met on the Wednesday and then the following Saturday they met again. She was impressed with this slight fellow with glasses, she just loved his studious look and she was really surprised when his mate Brian said that Philip was a great footballer. He didn't look at all like a footballer: he was way too thin and delicate-looking. But Brian was of similar build and he came with a reputation for being a tidy footballer as well. Grace's notion that all soccer stars had to be big and hunky was blown out of the water. She went to watch the summer factory league matches. Neilson's were playing Dougie Egbert's from Mullingar in the semi-final. Grace took a seat on the small wall behind the goal that Neilson's played into. Both Philip and Brian ran the show. Philip with his quick feet and Brian with his amazing skill, but it was a tight match and when it ended, one all thirty minutes' extra time didn't provide a decider, so it went to penalties. Brian took the first one and scored, so both teams went tit for tat until Mullingar missed one, then up stepped Philip – if he scored Neilson's were in the final – no problem to Philip, he puts the goalkeeper the wrong way, and he was chaired off the pitch by his teammates.

Six months later he asked Grace to marry him, though they had been only dating for less than a year. She said yes immediately and she started to cry and Philip hugged her steely until the sobbing ceased. They had full sex for the first time that night; but that wasn't to say they didn't have sex before, as they had often taken advantage of Brian's sojourns back to Cork to see his family. Sometimes it was awkward as Grace was nervous and Philip was all too eager so it always ended up as kissing and fondling, she playing with his penis and he massaging her breasts, and then trying to stimulate her clitoris. However, penetration didn't arise until the night he proposed. As luck would have it, Brian came home early from Cork, so they had sex in the back of his car, which he had left for the night in the side alley beside the lads' flat.

Grace often thought about it, that first night of penetration. She thought of the cat that jumped from the side wall unto the bonnet of Brian's car; it made her jump – it was a dirty, sleazy thing with scraggy fur and evil eyes, and she swore it stopped to stare at them.

Philip was overcome with her acceptance of his marriage proposal and when he removed himself from her he said gently, 'We have our whole lives ahead of us, Gracie.' She stayed quiet, thinking of what she had just done and then dreading that she might get pregnant; she had visions of walking up the aisle, her bump like a swollen football underneath her pure white wedding dress. But Philip's words soothed her.

'You know what I love about you, Gracie?'

'No.'

'You are so dark; you are native dark – your hair jet black – I love it long.'

'What else?'

'Your skin – on your face it is so soft.'

'My skin, you must be jokin – it's like sandpaper.'

'I like them too.'

He squashed her huge breasts with the palm of his left hand.

'What else?'

'You have a beautiful arse!'

Grace laughed.

'You are a really good footballer – and a nice man – you're a bit skinny and your glasses make you look a bit like John Lennon, but otherwise you'll do.'

Neilson's downgraded their Athlone operation so Philip was relocated back to Dublin. Grace was busy planning the wedding and at first any thoughts of relocating took a back seat. However, she could sense a change in Philip; he was down about it all and the only option with going back to Dublin was to move back in with his mother. He had very little savings. Grace only had her wages each week, and when that ran out, the next week's wages saved the day.

Philip was philosophical about it all and it was to his credit that after time he created a plan, and he cheered up: he concluded that his mother's place would give them time to save and consolidate. The old mother wasn't so bad, really, and her bark was worse than her bite; plus, she was lonely now as his two older sisters had married and moved on.

Grace wasn't sure; her own mother said that two women can't share the same kitchen, never mind mother and daughter-in-law. Her mother and then her father advised her to speak to Philip about renting a small flat in Dun Laoghaire, like somewhere near the Neilson's factory.

Philip didn't warm to the idea and he was sure that he could get Grace some kind of a job in the Neilson's, which would mean they would both be earning and saving; and soon they would get out of the Noggin, and get their own place – he argued that a flat is great, but the problem is not just the rent but the bills that go with it. He itemised it all out for her – electricity, coal or gas, food and other over-heads to do with maintaining gardens, etc.; in conclusion he was sure that returning to Sallynoggin was the only option.

The wedding was quiet if indeed weddings can be quiet. Philip didn't have a huge family, but of course both his sisters came with their respectives. Bridget had two children under seven and she was friendly; Marie was reticent like her mother and she was married for five years but childless. Grace had a bigger family and between herself and Helen they had lots of people to invite. Most of the staff at Miller's Drapery turned up and a few of her aunties and uncles came along; her father's sister, Aunt Nuala, came from London with her new partner, scandalising her mother, but then she saw her father laughing about it.

The day was quiet because the room was too small and it sort of condensed the crowd. The band was slow to start but once they got going, they got the crowd up. Philip was a music connoisseur; he loved The Rolling Stones and many obscure groups from America. She was hoping he would lighten up and enjoy the thrash on offer, but he spent most of the day attending to his mother, who was busy finding fault with all. The day went by so fast – Grace was exhausted at the end of it all; she sat on the bed whilst Philip used the bathroom and she chided herself because she had succumbed to his pressure about the honeymoon.

'We can have it later,' he said, 'when the finances are better – maybe we can go to Spain for a week; I hear Salou is great.'

She had agreed out of exhaustion, her acquiescence complete as she was complicit, telling all the guests of their plans – saying bland things, like, 'The sun ain't going nowhere, it will wait for us.' She perked up when she heard Philip return from the bathroom.

'It went great,' she said.

'It did.'

'Yer mother came around.'

'Eventually, why is it always about her?'

'I dunno – just the way she is.'

'Maybe – she doesn't mention my father for years, then when it comes to my wedding she breaks down in tears about him – now can you credit that – only for Marie intervening, she would have spoilt everything,'

'That's her way,' Grace said.

Philip stopped the conversation, looking at her spread across the double bed in her night dress.

'Here we are at last – just us on our wedding night. You look great – I was thinkin that earlier, how great you looked.'

'Thanks,' Grace chirped, going red.

She didn't mind the Noggin; it was as expected, big and sprawling, and fast with lots of lanes and back alleys, but in general the people were busy and friendly. Philip still liked to go to mass, so they met people through the church, and he still played football, so she went to watch him in all the home matches. She brought a brolly when it rained and a blanket when it was sunny; soon she got to know some of the other players and their girlfriends – only one or two players were married.

All in all, she settled in quite well, and she soon forgot about the disappointment of a honeymoon. She could see that Philip was saving regularly, so the dream was still alive, but she didn't get a job in Neilson's as one of Philip's neighbours got her a job in Tyler's, the medical suppliers up on Pottery Road. It wasn't rocket science: it was just a job on the assembly line, but the money wasn't bad and the women she worked with were all locals and full of the craic, and most of all it got her away from her mother-in-law.

Mrs Tynan ran the kitchen, which she reiterated was hers and hers only. She ran it with military precision; with Philip getting home first at 5:45 and Grace coming in around fifteen minutes later at 6:00, invariably dinner greeted Grace as she stepped into the small kitchenette.

Neither Grace nor Philip had any say as to what was on the menu – it was served up and that was it. She was never asked nor did she offer any opinion as to her favourites. The food was good, though – pork chops on Mondays with beef stew on Tuesdays in winter; in summer a salad with new potatoes. Wednesday was shepherd's pie in winter, chicken salad in summer – on Thursdays she left a casserole in the oven as it was the only day she went out.

Mrs Tynan took the bus to Dun Laoghaire and then she took the number eight to Dalkey to see her old friend Mrs Meagher. It was a huge commitment, winter and summer, as she had to get the two buses back home as well; Mrs Meagher was her work colleague from way back when she first arrived in Dublin. They had always kept in touch, alternating their visits until Mrs Meagher had an accident falling down the stairs at home, suffering extensive injuries which, after multiple surgeries, left her in a wheelchair. Mrs Tynan took it all in her stride stoically; she kept up the routine and the bus journeys for years.

Of course on Fridays they had fish – not that Grace liked fish, but you didn't get a say-so – so most weeks they had pan-fried white fish, but occasionally Mrs Tynan oven-baked hake and the odd time she stretched to smoked haddock, which Grace just left on her plate, passing her portion over to Philip when Mrs Tynan was busy at the sink. Otherwise Mrs Tynan was courteous and occasionally when Philip was at football she would break out the whiskey and the two women would sit at the kitchen table and chat.

'It's great all the same what they can do these days – sure the little mite wouldn't have stood a chance in my day.' She was referring to a premature baby that survived, defying all the odds – it was in the previous night's *Herald*.

Grace wasn't sure what to say as Mrs Tynan's wandering eyes made regular visits to her midriff, worryingly, it was like she was expecting a sudden large bump, followed by a glorious announcement; she never said anything, but Grace could sense the expectancy and even sometimes what she figured to be disappointment.

'Philip's late,' she said.

'I know, it goes on forever – here you finish that, Maura, ah go on I can't swallow it.'

'You'll kill me, dear,' but Mrs Tynan took the whiskey and lowered it down and it brought life to her face. Just for a second Grace caught a glimpse of her as she was when she was young; she had been pretty, not beautiful, but good-looking just the same.

'I'm worried about Philip,' Grace said suddenly, stopping cold, not fully believing that she had just said those words.

'Whatever's the matter?'

'He is restless – he is not sleepin – I wake up and he is wide awake just lying there and then he gets up for work and he is gone – I don't think he's slept for weeks.'

'Hasn't he?'

Grace looked at her intently. 'It not good.'

And then Mrs Tynan said, 'Nay, it's not, he best go get checked out!'

Philip did go to the doctor a few weeks later and after investigation he was diagnosed with a rare blood disorder that left him infertile and partially deaf, amongst many other minor but irritating things. The news of his infertility was devastating and when Grace got the news she took to the bed sobbing silently into her pillow. Philip sat at the kitchen table discussing his diagnosis with his mother, they drank endless cups of tea but when his mother enquired about Grace he passed it off; she was tired and upset by the news, and all she needed was a good sleep.

Philip never discussed his diagnosis with Grace – he passed it off, saying that adoption was the new thing, citing one of the office girls in Neilson's, who had adopted twins. Grace wasn't impressed but she kept quiet about it all – she felt sorry for Philip now – as her only thoughts were to having a baby, but meanwhile he had become profoundly deaf in his left ear, also he didn't look well and he was even paler and more delicate-looking than before. The doctor had given him tablets to help him sleep; they did help but all in all things had taken a turn for the worse.

Philip struggled on but soon he was advised to quit football as any injury would aggravate his condition, so they took to going up to the pub a few nights a week to get out – it was hardly a healthy replacement but at least Philip met some of his teammates after training. One of them, James Montgomery, was very keen on the idea of Philip becoming team manager for the new season. Grace was delighted he was asked as it would give him a new lease of life and keep him involved with the lads.

Philip was non-committal over deliberating and he was going on funny, confiding in her that he had lost interest in his football ever since his diagnosis, and now he was reviewing everything in his life. He proudly announced that he was non-religious: miraculously he announced that he no longer believed a word of it and he wouldn't be going to mass anymore – presumably that meant that Grace wouldn't be going to mass either as they always went together, not that she felt overtly religious – it was just something they did. Philip also announced that he had lost faith in his music, describing Mick Jagger as a false profit and John Lennon as a phoney and it was no wonder that he was shot. He was now into art-house movies like *Diva* – Philip was now a fully-fledged intellectual and he held court up in the Graduate pub, enlightening anyone who cared to listen to him, talking earnestly about this director and that director – and particularly about his favourite director, Sergio Leone.

Grace was bored by now. She was his constant companion even if sometimes it seemed to her that's all she was, his companion. Whether it was down to his infertility or not she didn't know, but Philip only took a ritual interest in her every Sunday morning when Mrs Tynan went off to mass and the front door slammed. He would turn to her – she could smell the previous night's drink; it stained the air around her; disgustingly, the corners of his lips still had dried Guinness stains; his mouth was stale and dry; it wasn't at all romantic – he would fiddle and fumble trying in vain to stimulate her by playing hard with her nipples, yet it was like his fingers had grown steel wool. Grace tried to respond but her reaction was dull and frigid – he dropped his left hand and rubbed between her legs till she got moist but it was involuntary, just like her body reacted but her mind was frozen.

Philip mounted her and forced his tongue into her mouth and she gasped for air and protested but he took this as a sign of willingness, but after a while he got fatigued and he stopped, exhausted; he just lay on top of her for a minute, his breathing erratic, but he was quiet like he was thinking about something. Grace didn't speak as this was his habit and it didn't seem to make any sense to change now. He withdrew from her, staying in the position on his knees, yet she instinctively knew what she had to do so she struggled to her knees, but the bed was creaky. Some of the springs were damaged; she listened to the grating noise of steel, the springs catapulting like an irregular heartbeat, and he waited till she was set, her head in the pillow, her hair fallen over wildly, to partly cover her face.

He entered her from the rear, starting off slowly but then steadily increasing the tempo the more that she backed into him, till at last he exploded with a deep growl and then he gave her one last thrust. He lay back, satisfied, and she lay beside him, holding back the tears.

Christmas became a favourite time as Grace got to go home for four or five days, giving her a chance to catch up with her mother and father, and most of all Helen, who was going out with a guard. By all accounts he was very handsome but he had a mean streak, evidently he wasn't shy with his fists when things went against him. Helen would often come home with bruises, but she was quiet about it even though her mother despaired and Grace's father hoped that Helen might confide in Grace as they had always been so close.

Philip came along out of duty. He didn't seem to mind so much as it gave him a chance to catch up with a few of his old football mates but Brian had gone back to Cork to be close to his aging parents. Grace was looking forward to meeting up with her younger sister; perhaps they might go out for a few drinks with Teresa Fay, not that Helen had ever liked Teresa that much, but Teresa was a great one for the craic and the jokes and famously it was said that she could bring a smile to anyone's face.

Philip tried one last time to engage her father about soccer, but her father loved the GAA so that conversion was nipped in the bud; understandably, Philip just went quiet and her father went into the kitchen to help with the dinner.

Helen looked well – she had no visible bruises and her guard was away home for a few days to see his folks.

'Where's he from?' Grace asked.

'Roscommon.'

'Muck savages,' Philip said, trying to be funny.

'His people are very respectable,' Helen said proudly.

'Animals,' Philip said suddenly.

'Who's animals?' Grace said.

'Guards.' Philip said, turning on the television; he was finished talking.

'Do you want me to do your hair?'

'Not now.' Helen moved, uncomfortable on the sofa. 'Maybe later on.'

The telephone rang and an hour later Philip and Grace sat on the Dublin train. Mrs Tynan had taken a turn and was in hospital. The medics said it was a minor stroke, yet with physiotherapy and rest she should make a full recovery.

Philip didn't say much about it and Grace felt that he was holding back, but they had a good weekend because the house was quiet, and for once she felt she could go to the kitchen whenever she pleased, or she could just sit on the sitting-room sofa and watch her favourite shows. Mrs Tynan was conspicuous by her absence and no matter how much Grace chided herself, she couldn't help wishing that Mrs Tynan would stay away for as long as possible – she was day-dreaming the medics might find a reason to keep her in hospital.

It was that weekend whilst drinking in the Graduate that she noticed that James Montgomery left his eyes with her just that little bit too long. When Philip was lecturing the crowd on football or politics James was staring at her, and when she looked back he suddenly dragged his eyes elsewhere but, alarmingly, she knew that he was glad to be caught. What was this now? He was about five years younger and James had plenty of girlfriends but he wasn't married yet. Maybe he was just flirting with her as he was a good friend of Philip's, but maybe he wanted something more and perhaps she did too. Soon Grace found herself staring back at him; it was so easy, she just held her gaze longingly for a few seconds outside of the norm.

This went on for weeks. Philip didn't notice and some-times both she and James were about to burst, as they were exhaustingly living a reality within a reality. She started to fantasise about him coming to the door when Philip was out bringing his mother to a medical appointment;

the thought of she and James making love on her marital bed – but he was so gentle and considerate, even though he was raw and willing, but he wanted only her and he kissed gently over her entire body. Then one ordinary night James wasn't there and someone said that he had met someone at work and they were going out. Grace's heart sank and she wondered why she gutlessly never made a move.

Two years after her mini-stroke Mrs Tynan had a massive stroke and she died. Philip found her on her bedroom floor – her head had smashed against the bedside locker and the carpet was ruined with blood. He cried for weeks afterwards, and he was rough with his sisters over the funeral arrangements and the will, which was about as basic as one would expect from a woman who had nothing.

There was no dispute about the house: Philip had bought it from the Corporation, paying for it monthly for three years before; he had another two years to go to secure the title deeds. But he was rough about her possessions, not trusting his sisters but particularly Bridget's husband, who worked in a solicitor's office.

'Have a word, Grace,' Marie pleaded on behalf of her sister. 'He has lost the run of himself if he thinks we want anythin of Mammy's – will you tell him? He won't listen to us.'

'I'll do my best,' Grace conceded.

'He'll listen to you – you are inseparable you go everywhere together; I've never seen a couple as tight.' Marie's words struck a chord.

Grace felt like shouting out, 'Have you any idea how bored I am – we do nuthin except go to the pub and watch these really boring films, and talk about politics and football! I'm ready to die, don't you see that?' But she didn't say a word, pragmatically, she just promised to have a word with her husband.

Now that Mrs Tynan was gone she said all to him in the kitchen and for once she felt like he was listening to her, mainly because he didn't interrupt as normal and he actually allowed her speak. When she had exhausted herself, he let go.

'You never liked my mother, did you? Always givin out, complainin about her – saying she was this and that – running her kitchen – do you know how many meals she cooked for you? Or the amount of washin she did? Not to mention the cleanin and tidyin, every single day of her life – now you're interferin with my bitch sisters – if yah think I am goin to let Alan Swain take me ma's furniture and the lousy few bob she had in savins, yah can go an fuck yerself.'

Grace was speechless – she watched helplessly as he slammed the kitchen door.

The family didn't fall apart over it all and the girls got their share, and indeed in fairness to Alan Swain he stayed out of it. Grace went with Philip every Sunday to tend the grave, but after time it became once a month and then once every six months, until eventually it was once a year and ritually on Christmas morning. Both Grace's parents had died by now and her sister Helen married the guard, who gave her two children. He still beat her from time to time, but she always said that it was her own fault and that she shouldn't be antagonising him.

Then Philip got a shock when Neilson's announced they were closing their Irish business, and all their staff was to be made redundant. In a way Grace was relieved as his overall health was suffering now; not only was his hearing impeded but his eyes were giving problems as well. He got ten thousand punts, redundancy enough to live on for a few years, so wisely he decided to pay off the last instalments on the house.

Grace was now the breadwinner as Philip was at home all day and it was very much a case of plodding along, and like Marie said they still went everywhere together, presenting the image to any onlooker that they were the perfect couple and very happy and content.

One day whilst walking home from work Grace crossed the playing fields just off of Rochestown Avenue, it leading to the Noggin and home. It was a dull misty afternoon after three solid days of rain. Dolefully, the Noggin houses looked small despite the lush gardens and their splendid array of hedgerows. The walls were dampened so they took deeper shades of pebbled grey and below, near the road, vagrant pools formed, and swish swash the gulls entertained themselves. Suddenly she heard plodding feet sinking in the grass behind her.

'How is yah?'

'James, I haven't seen you these years, where have you been?'

He came abreast of her.

'I've been away but I am back, as the man says – I tried marriage but it didn't suit me – so I am a free man again – as free as a bird, back in me ma's – you know me ma died?'

'It was a dreadful accident.' Grace stopped to look him over, concluding that he was still lovely in a boyish way, yet he was five years older than the last time she laid eyes on him.

'How's Phil?'

'Philip is himself – you know his ma died too?'

'I do – bad news finds a way.'

'So who's at home now?'

'Just Sallyanne – that's it, sometimes Derek if yer one throws him out – you know.'

'Derek, now there's a man.'

'You said it, Grace.'

'Are you workin?'

'Yeah – I'm out in Bray in the new toilet paper factory – I measure the sheets, you know if it says 180 sheets it's true because I measure them –' he laughed.

'Shut up.'

Grace stopped again when they reached the road.

'What's yer place like, Grace?'

'Fed up – same old, I wuldn't mind a change …'

'Let me know – I can get you in – just tell me whenever.'

He was walking away from her, so he turned around before walking backwards whilst gesturing with his hands:

'Not a problem – you look beautiful, by the way.'

He was gone, leaving her with the sounds of seabirds screeching in the sky.

That night she went to the Graduate with Philip but she never mentioned James – she surprised herself with her mood – her spirits were high, it was like James had injected her with something magical.

Grace took James up on his offer even though Philip was against it. He was going on about loyalty and change, and how she might not settle in at her new job, and then what? But Grace won the argument, saying that she would get an extra punt an hour, whilst urging Philip to put through his claim for disability now that his funds were getting low. The new job was better not just because of the money but mainly because she had more responsibility; it was an American company and they had lots of innovative ways of incentivising staff. They organised social events like bowling and nights out in Bray, and Dun Laoghaire, and somehow it was a totally different situation going out with her workmates and without Philip.

On this night they visited the amusements on Bray seafront before retiring to Royal Hotel for food and drinks. James was there and approached her with a newfound confidence, at once sitting beside her and taking her hand; he squeezed it gently whilst he chatted to her.

She was late home and Philip was up when she got in.

'You're late – what time do you call this?'

'I told you we were going out – we go out the last Friday of every month.'

'Think you'd be sick of the sight of each other.' He went to make tea but Grace followed him into the kitchen. 'My eye is actin up – I couldn't watch the telly – so I fell asleep on the couch.'

'I told you to get a new prescription for those eyes.'

'I know, but –'

She cut him short. 'James was there, he was askin after you.'

'That's crap, that fella walked out on his wife.'

'She was a bitch.'

'So he tells us.'

'What is it about you an James?'

'He ran out on his wife – he was probably havin affairs – are you goin to be this late every time you go out with that crowd?'

'I might,' Grace said, watching him drink his tea.

'I won't stand for it, Grace,' he said defiantly, but she just turned and walked out of the kitchen – she went up to bed noisily, stamping her feet on the stairs in protest.

Philip didn't go out much anymore. They only went to the Graduate the odd time, even though the lads were still nagging him about managing the team, but he always side-stepped the issue skilfully. Grace kept working to schedule, and putting her name forward for any of the social events that came up.

'How come you never bring me along?' Philip said to her one morning out of the blue. She was getting ready for work and he sort of caught her unawares.

'Nobody brings their husbands or wives – it's the way it is.'

'It's not enough that yah work with each other, yahs all want to ride each other too.'

'Don't be ridiculous.' She looked back at him; he looked so frail and delicate in the bed.

'I think you hate me,' he said pathetically.

'Hate you? Why would I hate you?'

'You just do – I know you do, whatever did I do to you?'

Grace wanted to tell him – she wanted to tell him that she was going to leave him, that she had made her mind up, and that her future was with James.

'If I hate you, Philip – it is you that taught me how to hate.'

He closed his eyes and she gently closed the bedroom door behind her.

The Posh Party

1975

Larkin dreamed regularly about a girl called Melissa, yet he wasn't sure if that was her real name. Dunne said her name was Alison and Murray said he really liked all the girls from that school as they all wore short tartan skirts with giant ornamental safety pins. Larkin was in love with his Melissa – it didn't matter what her name was, Melissa or Alison or Mary Anne – he just loved her beautiful long blonde hair that fell to her middle, and she had developed good breasts for a girl of sixteen and she hid them under a clean white blouse. She had everything, with pouty red lips and high cheekbones, and it was Dunne who said that she epitomised class and that she must have come from a long line of beauties. Murray reluctantly agreed, saying that she was well bred and it was so obvious that she came from money.

In many ways Murray was just trying to be helpful but

deep down Larkin knew what Murray was really saying, and it was bloody obvious he was just telling him to stop wasting his time, 'She's out of your league.' And she was. Despite Larkin's attempts to catch her eye on the bus home from school.

The girls were already ensconced by the time the bus got to Dun Laoghaire, three or four of them huddled at the rear of upstairs. One sitting sideways, her bare knees blocking the aisle, she had to correct herself to allow people to pass, not that it bothered her at all. Alison or whatever her name was usually sat on the back seat, allowing her a full view of the world. Larkin, copying the other girl, sat sideways on the inside, pretending to talk to Dunne soes he could just spin round to Murray, and then move his eyes slowly down the bus over the heads of coughing oul wans and smoking oul lads just to see her holding court – she was so beautiful.

When she stepped off the bus at the top of the Noggin Hill he watched her part company with her friends. His face stuck to the cold glass of the window. He dreamed of her, imagining her house all ordered; she had a suited professional father and a serious but doting mother. At first she was an only child but then he added an equally lovely sister, who at first was older, but then out of decency he made her just a little younger. He wandered into Melissa's bedroom, which was neat and tidy with nice lace curtains on the window. She had soft toys strewn against her pillow with lots of books, and on top of them copies of *Jackie*. He saw her sitting on the bed before standing and changing from her school uniform, imaging her body and no matter how many times he imagined her, the image was always the same: his camera moved down the curves of her hips, focusing on her behind. Larkin played with his pictures so as in one shot her bottom was robust, but in another it was petit and narrow.

'Yes, this was his fixation.'

Seanie stopped writing. He was confused, as everything that Larkin did he had done himself. He was Larkin – Larkin fancied the same girls as him and made the same astute calculations as him: yes, they shared a life. Larkin was better-looking though, or was he? Come on now, to be fair, Larkin was a bit of everyone. It all reminded him of Mr Mullins, his English teacher, when he said nobody does anything if nothing happens – so he kept having things happen to Larkin. In his story Larkin didn't know the girl's name, but in real life Seanie knew she was Alison McCann. And she was posh, from a well-off family, and she was beautiful to go with it. She did get off the bus at the top of the Noggin Hill – but all of those girls were beautiful, including her cousin, Dr Ryan's daughter, she that lived in the big house with the orchard, over the high wall, the physical boundary that marked that side of the Noggin, whereas on the other side where Murray lived, it was the fairways of Dun Laoghaire Golf Club. But Larkin shared his fascination with blonde girls that were inherently good-looking, also he had himself sore masturbating over her. It would explain why the shaft of his manhood was so sore – jerking off over Alison McCann day after day, trying to get her arse image right. Seanie was being disingenuous, mind you, as Mr Mullins was referring to the IRA and their campaign; like he used to say stuff like, 'If everyone stayed at home and did nothing, then nothing would happen and there would be no news, so everything would stay the same, boys – just as it is, people only react to action – you can spout all the brilliant words you want but it's action that stirs people.'

'Does he control Larkin?'
'Not really, he feels that sometimes Larkin controls him.'

Seanie wanted to make Larkin into something and he wanted him to be wise and not full of angst. Larkin was the one who tried to figure out things, stuff like why Frank Mooney had two hundred and seventy 45s. Why did Liam Devine put snails in the kids' bags at Halloween? And how was it that Terry Murphy would either have lockjaw or he would just die after this culchie lashed a sliother at him for not getting out of the way down the footballers? Terry Murphy was playing soccer, just a game of three and in, at the Gaelic posts. Along comes a 'muck savage', from God knows where, and when he tells Terry and his buddies to get out of the way – they refuse as they were there first – so yer man gets his hurley and lashes the sliother into Terry's gob. Thus the lockjaw and then the possibility of imminent death. Now why can't Larkin tell stories like that, why does he have to be so intense about women, and his school sweetheart in particular? He could enlighten us with tales of sneaking over the wall into Dr Ryan's orchard, stealing apples, and how Philomena O'Neill stuffed them down her knickers. Oh no, Larkin would have to fall in love with 'Ryan's daughter'. Maybe it was for the better that he kept Larkin so close to him. Larkin was his get out, because if Larkin said it, well, it was Larkin, not Seanie; it was all Larkin's thoughts, his doing, and Seanie was in no way responsible.

Then one day Alison, Melissa or Mary Jane looked up at him, and it was one of those soft days when the rain stuck in one million adhesive dots on the bus window. Murray wiped the glass with his sleeve rolled up to cover his fist. Dunne was singing 'Hand Me Down My Bible' by the Dubliners – the bus was unusually empty – and on this day she was with one other girl and it was the girl who crossed her legs blocking the isle, but she wasn't getting off for another stop. Larkin watched Melissa as she said goodbye to the aisle girl and set on down the stairs. Larkin copied Murray by wiping the window, it was magic as soon he could see and there she was, he watched as she stepped onto the pavement. The bus shuddered, then, taking a final breath, made to go. Larkin wiped the window again fast – and she went to walk on but suddenly she looked up. Heave; the bus thrust away and their eyes met. She stayed looking till he finally lost sight of her.

Murray was laughing, he shouted, 'Yer in der boy!'

And Dunne stopped singing the Dubliners. 'You've cracked it,' he said, 'yer made.'

'Larkin felt the flow of warmth, that feeling he felt only when it was his birthday; he carried it on home with him.'

When Seanie realised that he was never going to be with Alison McCann he swore to himself that Larkin would. It wasn't a way of seeking retribution or getting her back as she didn't do anything, save she was just aloof and because in effect she never saw Seanie's angst. To her, Seanie was just another kid on the bus, he was general public; he was alright making up the numbers as long as one didn't have to mix with him, or have to engage with him on a personal level. Now this analysis was only true on one level as some of these posh girls would deliberately wanna be working class and some of them even developed the accents and demeanours to go with it. Walking around the streets of the Noggin with the hardchaws, this was how they practised their commonality; these girls, as it was only girls, usually had a gripe against their parents or were delinquent for some other reason. But Seanie couldn't put Alison into that bracket as she was altogether just too sweet and too posh.

So when Larkin was invited to a party he knew she was to attend he was delighted and excited and, more importantly, shit scared. Him at a party over in Bellevue, would he stand out like a sore thumb? The aisle girl said, 'You should come – we'll all be there.'

'What about me mates?' Larkin asked.

'Yeah, that's cool, but don't bring anyone else; we don't want any trouble – my mother is going to loads of trouble for my birthday.'

'There was no booze allowed but you could tank up before you went.

Larkin was already stupefied just thinking about it all.'

Seanie was feeling sheepish now as he was basing most of this on his own invite to Claire Kirwan's party. He really fancied Claire but she was boyfriend-friendly with normally two or three serious punters a year. Word was that she did the trick, put it out, but only with carefully selected boys. Seanie knew her through her brother Joe; he was an ineffectual lad who was always friendly but in an exploratory way – it was like this is the world and the world expects me to do this, so I had better do it – so he hovered on the periphery of all rather than made any real contribution. They were part of the gang that hung around in the Horse & Hound in Cabinteely.

Seanie latched on to Claire for two reasons: one, that she had this wonderfully interesting face, and two, because she was flawed. Seanie loved flawed. She had a dark tooth when she smiled and you could see its discolour, it was green like the sea, but this was the makings of her. It was her eighteenth and she was meeting friends and others in the Horse and there was serious talk of going to a nightclub in Bray later.

Of course Murray said he couldn't go, well, he wasn't sure, which usually meant that it was a definite no. But Dunne was up for it and he produced a condom from his back pocket and handed it to Larkin.

'Where did yah get dat?' Larkin said.

'Mind yer nose now, I have my ways.'

By the time Larkin removed Dunne's big face from his own, he had deposited the condom in his pocket and he got a sudden rush of adrenalin – what if?

Maybe, who knows?

Some of those posh girls go for it; it's a way for them to reject poshness – all they want is to be safe, they don't wanna have to bring up any old kid – no, these girls are saving their wombs for professional types but hey they love to experiment and live close to the edge and get lots of wedding-night practice. Larkin was sure he was right and he could have kissed Dunne.

'Where did yah get it?' he asked once again.

Dunne went to thrust his big head into his face once more so Larkin withdrew.

Dunne, wondering what Larkin was thinking about, just tapped his nose.

'I don't have three older bruthers for nuthin,' and Larkin accepted this and beamed on.

Dunne stopped for a second. 'Is dat de front door?' He jumped from the battered armchair and ran to the small window. The street outside was empty. 'Someone selling sumthin, can't see anyone, thought me ma was home early; nah she wudn't mind yah, Larkin, but she hates Murray.'

'Dat's cause he's a wanker.' Larkin got out of his chair like he was about to go; soes Dunne just looked him up and down, but he didn't say anything.

'His ma won't let him go to de party,' Larkin said triumphantly.

'He might 've to mind his little sister,' Dunne added appeasingly.

'She's big enough to mind herself,' Larkin said, still attacking.

'Yer right, he is a wanker.' Dunne grinned.

'Why would Larkin loved flawed, you would swear he thought of bleeding pigs?'

Seanie was staring into her mouth so much that Claire stopped talking for a minute; irritated, she was about to say something to him, but Carter, her latest boyfriend, said, 'Dug in – I can take three of yahs.' He wasn't speaking to Seanie but to the whole crowd, who counted seven. 'Davis has his oul wan's car, and he doesn't drink.'

'Yes, he does,' Carter said, standing up, showing off his new leather jacket.

Seanie thought that Carter was a rat, like he had a rodent head and his ears were too big for him.

'He does drink – but not when he's drivin the oul wan's car,' Seanie said to Claire, who was concentrating on keeping her mouth closed.

'Whatever the fuck,' Carter said. 'Who am I takin?'

'Me, I hope,' Claire said.

'Me too,' Seanie added.

'I can't bring fuckin all of yah.' Carter sat down again. He took a swig of his lager, leaving just a drain at the bottom.

'Davis is drivin,' Seanie said sternly.

'How de fuck do you know?'

'Cause he'll drive if I ask him,' Seanie said confidently.

'I'll believe it when I see it,' Carter said smugly, but as it so

happened Davis walked by and Seanie, seizing his chance, said, 'Give us a lift to the Dug?'

'Sure,' said Davis, shaking his mother's car keys.

Carter just grinned sardonically.

Claire looked on at Seanie like she was happy he had put Carter in his place – she went to say something, flashing her stained tooth, but her friend Becky Ruane came over screaming.

'Happy birthday – I love your hair, wow, you look great – we're only getting here, James was in town at a stag but I pulled him out of it.' She laughed with a cackle, even throwing her head back so as she was looking at the ceiling.

'We're goin to the Dug.'

'Jasus,' Becky said, studying Claire for a reaction. 'Have we time for a pint? I'm gasping.'

'Make it a quickie,' Claire said, and then she added, 'Is James driving? We're short of cars although Davis might have room.'

'James is stupefied – I'll go and ask Davis.'

'He'll have room for you and James … he is just gone out to the jacks.'

Seanie wanted to impress Becky but even though he was offering her a lifeline she ignored him completely.

'Will he bring us?' she asked Claire.

'I'll ask him when he comes back,' Claire said and Becky left to go to the bar.

Not only did Murray turn up but he had the money for drink as well. Dunne was impressed; he encouraged Murray go into the Graduate off-licence to get the flagons. Murray got the drinks no problem, but then he and Larkin had an argument about where to go to drink it. Larkin wanted to go down to the woods so as they could just nip around to the back of the church and be right beside the party in Bellevue. Murray pulled rank, though, he was going on about buying the drink, but only because he had paid for the booze he should have the shout on where to go to drink it; he wanted to go to the big rock on Mullos Hill.

'Fuck it,' Dunne said.

'It's not dat far.' He was looking at Larkin, who couldn't hide his disgust.

'How many bottles did yah get?' Dunne asked; Murray was holding the bag closed so as nobody could see.

'I got us a flagon each – an don' forget yah fuckers owe me.'

'Come on – we'll go by de Golf.'

Murray was pleased that Dunne had supported him so he lit a cigarette and he gave Dunne one, which was a cool move as Larkin didn't smoke.

Murray held the swinging gate open. The evening was settled; the sky was red and yellow over the Dublin mountains. When they turned to go up the grass track that ruptured the golf course, Dunne said, 'Ah fuck, der at it again.'

Murray said, 'Who?' but Larkin could see the smouldering black of a gorse fire and as they walked on he got that sweet sickly smell.

'Fuckers, like we go up here, rite, an we've a few flagons, but we don't make a mess – like do we, dat's why we bring de bag – dose fuckers jus wanna ruin everythin lightin fires like!' Dunne addressed Murray.

'Yeah,' Murray said like he had just been privy to some great wisdom.

'I doubt if dey start tem deliberate like,' Larkin volunteered.

'How's dat?' Dunne turned on him.

'Dey throw der bottles into de ferns – den wen its sunny dey catch fire like, the glass explodes wit de heat – get it.'

'Fuckers for throwin der bottles in de ferns den!'

Dunne pushed open the gate and they each held their hands out straight to negotiate the briars and the wild hedge on either side. Murray led the way. Dunne marched after him like he was watching the drink so there wouldn't be any accidents. Larkin was taken with the dried-out pond where he used to find frogs when he was a child. There was still a tiny trickle but nothing like there was years ago. Murray shimmied up the side of the rock and Dunne tried to do the same but he was too tall so eventually he had to use his hands and crawl. Larkin walked up in one fast go to the amazement of his companions.

They sat staring over the lower estates of Killiney, Ballybrack, all the way to Cornelscourt and Cabinteely.

'Look at de Noggin Church,' Dunne said; he always said that whenever they climbed the rock.

'Just tink, we are gonna walk all that way later in search of minge!'

Murray was opening his bag to share out the flagons.

'You mean Larkin's search for minge, I've no need!'

Murray handed Dunne his flagon and he fiddled in his pocket for his penknife but, despite his attempts at precision, the cider gassed out and down the sides onto his pants.

'Fuck it,' he said, 'I'm always doin dat.'

'Dat's cause yer a dope!' Murray took advantage of Dunne's preoccupation with his trousers.

Dunne gave him a look and that was enough to render Murray quiet, but Larkin said, 'Yah won't be allowed in; de girls will all tink dat yah pissed yourself!'

'Yeah,' Dunne said sarcastically, whilst resting on his elbow and holding his flagon tight, save that he might spill any more.

'Actually Larkin would have loved that band, he had a particular liking for live music.'

The band was called Ice Cube International, and the lead singer was a solid, good-looking fellow with a really good voice. Seanie sat at the bar with Davis, who was sipping a pint of orange. The song was called 'Military Man' – it was slow and melodical. Seanie watched Claire and Becky waving their hands in the air; they were part of the dark crowd that were glued together on the dance floor. Carter was sitting smugly at the far side of the bar: he was talking to James, who was swishing his pint dangerously in the air.

The music faded and Davis said enthusiastically, 'Good band.'

Seanie acknowledged him: 'Class.'

The band launched into another song – this was faster and

the dark crowd responded, the glue dissolving so soon Claire and Becky were dancing in space. Carter was the worse for wear and Seanie wondered how he would drive the car home, especially with Claire in it. He didn't mind what he did to himself but worried for Claire, who was beaming now, dancing in the spotlight with her friends surrounding her. The good-looking singer introduced his next song with, 'Happy Birthday, Claire Kirwan.' The place erupted with Claire's friends screaming. Seanie noticed that even people they didn't know were clapping and cheering.

'Can I get a lift back with you?' Claire asked Davis.

'Who else?' Davis asked soberly. 'I can only take three.'

'Dunno, probably just Becky and James?'

'What's wrong with Carter?' Seanie was really trying to point out that he was pissed.

'He has to work with his da in the mornin – he wants to leave his car here, he says his uncle is bringin him home – they're decoratin a shop on Main Street in the morning, so they can slip down and get it.'

'Oh,' Seanie said, not sure as to why he was happy, 'so you're comin back with us?'

'Yeah, if Davis can fit me in?'

Even in the low light Seanie could see the dark tooth and then he wondered was he drunk and did he just imagine it.

'I will be back in a minute – I just wanna say goodbye to them all.' Claire was gone. Seanie was glad, as it gave him some time to draw breath.

'Is yer oul wan still away?'

Davis looked back at him peculiarly, 'She's not my oul wan, Seanie – she is my mudder – Mater or Mags to you!' Seanie didn't know what to say but when he examined Davis's expression, he just laughed, and Davis laughed too.

'Bring us in for a coffee will yah — Becky and James will get out at the Brack.'

Once again Davis gave him a peculiar look. 'Don't stain the sofa.' And he laughed, but Seanie didn't as Claire was coming towards him.

'Great night,' Becky said from the rear.

'Great band,' Seanie said from the front.

'No good for dancing dough,' Becky said to Claire, ignoring Seanie.

'They're for listening to!' Claire told her.

'Listenin is not dancing, is it?'

'No,' Claire agreed, 'but I loved it just the same — the Dug is getting better!'

'Yeah,' Becky allowed. 'Will I wake him?' James was asleep, his head resting on her shoulder with his big mouth open and he was snoring loudly when the conversation went quiet.

'Leave him,' Davis demanded, like he was the captain of the car.

'He is always asleep, even when he is walking around chatting to us all — isn't that right, Seanie?' Seanie wanted to agree but he didn't want to be mean so he just grunted.

Claire and then Becky laughed, 'Yer right there, Davis, I spend my life tryin to wake him up.' Things went quiet from there on — Seanie busied himself watching all. In Shankill a few cars were moving slowly away from Byrne's pub. The white-washed walls stood out in the dark. All was quiet as they passed the ghostly St Anne's Church.

'Me ma got married in der!' Becky said to nobody, but Claire replied, 'Did she?'

'She did,' Becky went on, 'twenty-five years ago now.'

Becky woke the disoriented James and they got out at Wyattville. James made a sort of muffled sound of thanks before staggering his way to the footpath.

'See yis all! Drive safe, Davis.' Becky slammed the door shut.

'Fancy a coffee?' Davis said innocently.

Seanie waited anxiously for Claire's 'Yeah, why not, it's my birthday!'

'Been der seen it an Dunne it!' Murray said, sitting on the wall. 'How much 've yah left, Dunne?'

Dunne took another long swig.

'Yah 've loads left, Larkin, yah cunt!' Murray shouted. 'He's holdin back in case he gets a ride!'

'Fat chance.' Dunne was laughing.

Murray was waving his flagon as he spoke.

'Yah wudn't know wit Larkin – mainly because he looks like a girl, acts like a girl – he is …'

'A bitch!' Murray couldn't contain his laughter but Larkin, ignoring them as best he could, drank a right mouthful of cider, leaving just about a quarter left in the flagon.

'Wooh,' Dunne said.

'Woooh,' Murray said after him.

'Fuck off,' Larkin said, 'I don't wanna be pissed walkin up to de door.'

'Wat's yer women's name?'

'Who?' Larkin asked.

'Yer one havin de party?' Murray gave him a vicious look but then laughed just as quick.

'Dunno,' Larkin said, 'Vivian, or sumthin.'

'Great,' Dunne complained, 'we're invited to a posh party; we don't know de girl's fuckin name – brilliant.'

'I'm tired, lads,' Murray sat up on the wall, checking if he had disturbed anyone in the house behind him. 'It's a walk down here from Mullos.'

'Do you hear him?' Larkin said.

They had walked back by the Golf Club and down the lane before crossing over and walking on down Avondale Road. Dunne was leading the way; he turned into Bellevue and on by Sion Road, till Sallynoggin Church came into view. Murray suggested they wait around the corner from the birthday party just to finish the flagons. It was his only good idea. Just then two fellas from the Presentation College came along; they had bottles of coke; the taller one, who Larkin knew as Williams, slowed almost to a stop. Larkin knew him from the bus – he was a tall skinny fellow with a long crooked nose, who came to notoriety because he was the first bloke of their age to smoke a pipe publicly, and it was only tobacco he smoked. Larkin felt that Williams only engaged in it so as he would look intelligent and posh.

'How yahs, lads, ar yis goin to de party?' Larkin asked.

'We are,' said Williams, relaxing a little. 'We're running late,' he added, so as they wouldn't think he had time to hang around. 'See you got some cider – we tried to get some over in Dalkey, but the fucker in the off-licence threw us out.'

'Yah need Murray here – he looks older dan his granda,' Dunne said.

'Hey, what's yer women's name?' Murray asked.

'Who?'

'Yer wan havin de party,' Murray said, exasperated.

'Are you invited?' Williams's companion said, all officious-like.

'We fuckin are,' Murray said, sliding down from the wall.

'Ah, no problem,' Williams interjected, 'Viola Sweeney.'

'Viola?' Larkin said, 'Jasus, can yah play her – sounds like a violin, doesn't it?'

'Yeah, it does,' Williams said, pushing his friend along.

'Seanie thinks Larkin would have done better, but historically Larkin never achieved better outcomes.'

Davis made coffee and then he went to bed like the good thing that he was, and he never told a soul, he just disappeared, leaving Seanie and Claire alone in the living room. The sofa was big and Davis had even left on the glow of the gas fire. Seanie reminded himself to turn it off when he was leaving. Claire looked for Davis or rather listened for him a couple of times before she finally accepted Seanie's assertion that he had indeed gone to bed.

'He does that – sometimes he falls asleep standing up – he tries to avoid that.'

Claire laughed, sinking back in the sofa and, when she did, she exposed the strength of her breasts.

'Why do you stare at me, Seanie?'

He wasn't expecting her to say that.

'Do I?'

'Yes, you do.'

'I must like you so.'

'You must, but do you have to stare?'

'No – I don't have to.'

'Like I don't mind you liking me – but the staring kind of freaks me – you know?'

'Sorry.'

'You know I have this funny tooth – but believe me I wanted rid of it, but the dentist wouldn't hear of it – so I am stuck with this awful tooth – you seem fascinated by it?'

'No – I barely notice it.'

'It makes me ugly, doesn't it – you would really go for me if I had normal teeth; I know that.'

'Ah no – if anything I think it makes you even more attractive – to be honest.'

'Really?' Claire lifted herself forward to be level with him. 'How could that be – it's disgusting?'

'What does Carter think of it?' Seanie said softly.

'He never notices it – believe me, Seanie – I could have a face transplant and he wouldn't notice – Carter loves his da, drink, and his work in that order.'

'He is mad!'

'Why?'

'He just is ... because you're beautiful.'

She touched him with her moist lips and he submitted to her

tongue, and then he fed her his tongue but he withdrew when he felt it brush against her discoloured tooth, wondering was it infectious; maybe he might wake up and find all of his own teeth discoloured.

'I dunno if I wanna have sex?'

It wasn't the furthest thing from Seanie's mind but it didn't seem imminent either.

'I had sex with Carter this afternoon after his work – we went for a drive up the Sally Gap – we did it in the back of his da's Hiace.'

'Wow,' was all that Seanie could say.

'You probably – wouldn't find that too polite, Seanie, would you, having sex with someone who has already had sex? And I know what you think of Carter.'

'Well I dunno – suppose it wouldn't bother me really – but only if you are cool about it, Claire?'

'Carter gave out to me for farting during it – I can't help it, Seanie, every time I get aroused I fart – it just comes out kind of natural like ...'

Seanie coughed.

'We all have to fart, Claire.'

'That's what I said to Carter.'

It wasn't like the passion died or he fancied her any the less, but something broke within his imagination – it was like a giant gorilla had broken through the cage that imprisoned all of his fantasies.

'Come on, Claire – I'll walk you home.'

'So – it's not happening, then?'

'Hello, boys,' Mrs Sweeney said, studying each of them in turn to see if they had a present. She continued smiling but also continued to block the way with her arms.

'Viola.'

And the aisle girl from the bus appeared. She looked really well: she had permed her mass of curls and the makeup she wore had performed miracles, sharpening up her eyes.

'Grand,' she said, and her mother released her barrier arms.

'She's in the kitchen,' Viola whispered to Larkin as he walked by. Dunne looked ridiculous and out of place in this bright posh house, but Murray, with his mop of curls, could have passed for anything and he immediately started to chat to a group of girls at the bottom of the stairs.

The kitchen was huge – over in the far corner a couple of serious types were talking about the IRA. The girls they were with abandoned them to sit on the patio by the French windows. Williams and his pompous buddy were out there too; Williams whispered something when he saw Larkin, with Dunne towering behind him.

Larkin scanned the room for Melissa, but she wasn't there and his heart sank.

'Love your denims,' a random girl passing said.

'Are they Doc's?' she said on the way back.

Dunne poured himself a glass of coke and just leaned against the wall under the kitchen clock.

Then Melissa appeared from the garage with some tall fella wearing a blazer.

She pretended not to know Larkin so he wanted to run to Dunne for comfort.

'She loves you,' Viola said. Larkin turned round and he was taken with how well she looked close up, and he was making a mental note as she made for quality seconds. He moved towards Dunne but now he was talking to the smallest girl in the room, a petite thing with hair the length of her back.

Then Murray came in with this skinhead type – she had pins through her eyebrows and studs in her nose and chin.

'Who's he?' Larkin pointed at the tall fellow with Melissa.

'That's Tom – he's her cousin – go over to her.' Viola was gone; her mother needed her assistance at the front door.

Larkin walked over purposely and as he got near Melissa she turned her back on him deliberately, which left him facing Tom.

'Yes?' Tom smirked.

'Yes, I wanna talk to her!'

'Really – can't you see she's busy?'

'No – I just wanna say hello like.'

Melissa couldn't contain herself; she turned slightly, peeping over her shoulder.

'You want to talk to him?' Tom said, smiling broadly.

Melissa turned fully and Larkin knew why he had gone to so much trouble.

'It's alright, I do know him,' she said softly.

'You like a bit of rough so!' Tom said, but he winked at Larkin and went to join the serious fellows over in the corner. Larkin eyed him till he sat down and then he noticed that Murray was head-to-head in conversation with Viola's mother.

'I didn't think you would come – you or your mates.'

'Why?'

'Didn't think it was your kind of thing?'

'Surprise yah so.'

'Did you bring any drink?'

'No – we drank a few flagons dough.'

'Some of them have vodka in the coke bottles … I didn't bother – my parents are away and I know where the key is so I can just slip next door.'

'Dat's genius,' Larkin studied her eyes for clues.

She was warm towards him, he knew. 'I like you on the bus – you stare at me but I don't feel like you're a pervert – it's more like you stare at me the right way.'

'I don't mean to stare at yah – yer just so beautiful.'

'Yes, I am,' she laughed. 'How's about we slip away from my cousin and go have a drink?'

'Fine – sounds good.' Larkin followed her out the back and down the side of the house. She lived two doors up and, once inside, the house had a cold, empty feel.

'Gin, whiskey, beer – I am going a vodka because we have loads of vodka; the parents won't miss it too easily, you?'

'Beer maybe – 've yah enough?'

'Yeah – my father doesn't drink beer – he just has it for his friends when they come over.'

She handed Larkin a bottle of harp, leaving the cap on a silver tray.

'Do you drink much?'

'Flagons an me oul wan's Guinness, not dat she drinks Guinness, but like yer sayin she gets it for visitors.'

'I see, why don't you come over and sit beside me?'

Larkin did as she asked but up close she was fuller and heavier than he had imagined.

Her thick lips tasted like rubber, and somehow they reminded him of the condom he had stashed in the rear pocket of his jeans. She wanted to kiss him endlessly and she only paused to get more vodka. Strange she didn't offer him another beer, nor did he ask out of politeness. She kissed him for an hour till his lips were sore – and he was getting very tired of his come-and-go erections. Then suddenly she was rubbing his penis from the outside of his crotch.

'Do you want to ride me?'

She was breathing heavily so he turned his head to avoid inhaling her breath.

'I wanna make love to yah,' he said, trying to be clever.

Melissa paused, then helped herself to more vodka.

'Let's go up to bed then.'

He watched her undress.

She was big around the hips and she had multiple bruises down her thighs and shins.

'Hockey,' she said, pointing to one large bruise.

'Got a few like dat from football.'

'Rugby – no, you wouldn't play rugby?'

'No – we play football.'

'I brought my drink up.' She drank most of her glass down and then lay flat on the bed.

Her breasts were mountainous and Larkin just wanted to stand and admire her: nothing else seemed appropriate.

'Wat bout protection, I've a condom?' He wanted to sound grown up.

'No need – I am having my period.' She was matter of fact, then, turning on her side she went pale, and for one awful moment he thought she was about to vomit.

'Are you ok?' he asked, moving nearer the bed.

'I think I am gonna get sick.'

'Larkin agreed with Seanie that at the end of the day, women were made of blood and guts, just like men, and there was no pointing in pretending they were anything else.'

Seanie walked her to the top of Rochestown Avenue and when she was gone he got over the small wall of the Victor Hotel; walking on down through the parked cars, he felt suddenly alone.

The night porter went and got him twenty Major; he lamented another stupid attempt to quit gone by the wayside. However, inhaling the smoke on the last leg of the journey gave him comfort. He passed the milk man, who was crossing the street to go down the cul de sac but he was so intent on his work that he didn't see Seanie walk by. How Seanie loved the early morning, this bright new day with just the crows for company – better still was the thought of his warm bed despite his usual cold pillow, and the mulling over of a fantasy that was now dead.

'She puked, I don't believe yah,' Murray said.

'Wus der much blood?' Dunne asked.

'Took me ages ta clean up de puke, dose posh birds ar some pukers.' Larkin joined them to make it three astride.

'Wat bout de blood?' Dunne asked, 'Did yah get it on yer lad?'

'He had a fuckin condom,' Murray said.

'Never gotta out,' Larkin said mournfully.

'Yah mean yah sat der watchin her ballock naked, dying for it, an yah never rode her?'

Dunne was so cross he stepped out unto the road to distance himself.

'It wasn't like dat; wit puke everywhere in her hair an all over her tits – and blood seepin onto de sheets, der wus no way, lads – yis didn't exactly set de world on fire yerselves?'

'Wat?' Dunne said, 'I've a date wit dat small one wit de long hair … Joy. Murray nearly got off wit de mother only yer one Viola came in de bedroom an fucked Murray out …'

'Yeah,' said Larkin, 'an pigs fly.'

They walked on towards Honeypark to Murray's house, and they were swallowed by the dawn's early light.

David's Room

2016–1977–1968

I wake to the smell of flowers, yet there haven't been flowers for so long so I realise that I have been dreaming. Sitting upright in the bed, my head spins; I look at the medication on the bedside locker, then I cough uncontrollably. Drinking water from a glass that is too small, it empties quickly and I have another coughing fit. Glad I quit the cigarettes, but when the coughing eases I am no longer happy about that, in reality I am sorry. Remembering it is Thursday; Anna is coming to clean the house. On one hand I am happy she is coming, but on another it annoys me – with my cough and my head I would rather stay in bed. Anna is coming, I have to get up, but it is cold and I don't want to get up until my head stops spinning. Fixing the glass, I left it too close to the edge; when I move, it obscures my view of Lilly. I try to see her through it but she is distorted, so I move the glass beyond the frame. There she is. That photograph was taken on the final night of the 'Pirates', in the town hall in Dun Laoghaire. She was forty-six that year, I remember, because I was fifty and the four-year age difference was a standing joke between us. Funny how people who are dead still look so alive in photographs, isn't it? Strange to think that a body has withered to dust, but still looks fine and healthy sat there right in front of you – she was good that night; her cheeks were full red and her little button eyes looked upon me kindly.

Better not dawdle, Anna will come knocking. She takes over the house for the hour and I have to keep moving from room to room, lifting my feet to allow the noisy hoover sweep by the hearth. I wonder what Lilly would make of Anna, she wouldn't know where Latvia was, well, she would but she might have to look for it on a map. Imagine if I had told Lilly that night in the town hall that I would be left alone with a Latvian cleaner. She either would have laughed her head off or cried. Lilly really didn't care for fuss.

We had people in occasionally for the musical evenings. When she played the piano and I tried to sing, 'Ah go on, John, give us a song,' yet there were better singers than me, who never sang as they were too shy but it was no bother to her to play the piano mind. I could sing anything as long as I didn't go mad or go too high, I was grand. James Whelan, now he had a great voice, but he didn't like to sing and his wife Marion had a real sweet voice but she sang too low so people started to talk over her, which was a terrible shame. No amount of coughing and sshing worked. Sean Cassidy had the best voice though. He could really sing although his wife Irene didn't sing a note; she would listen to him passionately. Sean could play the piano too and he was funny with it. I liked him the best even though Lilly wasn't over-fond of his wife, who she said was stuck up.

I struggle out of the bed. The carpet is old and worn so it retains no heat. The bathroom is worse, the tiles are like ice, and the cold water from the tap startles me – I reckon that it tries hard to cure me, yet it is very harsh. I dress hurriedly, all of the time waiting for the key to turn in the front door, Anna looking up at me from the hall. I open the curtains to see out: the street is empty – a line of green bins stand uniformly outside of each house save for mine. I forgot to put mine out, still not too late but I want to make tea and eat before engaging in anything strenuous.

However, I am anxious, so I go out the back to get the bin. The grass is too long and the leaves have clogged the fenced run where I used keep King. The leaves are wet, sticking like transfers to the grass, and twits and house martins are chirping their endless sound, they are like a drill stop-starting. The heavy bolt on the back door requires all of my strength. Me dragging the bin through the narrow passageway. I have to adjust to fit it through the gap by the car; the car looks lonely as it hasn't moved for so long. As I place the bin against the railing I hear the deep sound of the bin truck coming down the road. Sean Cassidy's voice comes into my head and he sings the Ave Maria. I return to the back gate, sliding the bolt across, and it's funny as it closes so easily but it was so hard to open.

I feel cold when I boil the kettle but it isn't cold out. I am thinking of the leaves choking the garden and sticking to the street. All of the gullies are clogged, and the hedges are doing their damnest to hide all. The tea is strong – it warms me but I am still hungry. I don't think I will have time to cook before Anna arrives. I don't know what it is, I have never been able to eat properly when there are people about. I leave it; plenty of time to eat when she leaves. The phone rings, it is Anna and she babbles on: she has slipped whilst waiting for the bus, twisting her left ankle; she can't put any weight on it. She apologising fervidly. Looking at the wall clock I realise that she should be here by now. I tell her not to worry, that the house will do till next week. She says she will ring me on Monday to let me know how the ankle is, and if she will be alright to come next week. I say that is grand and put the phone down. Now for food.

I survey the house in my head. Knowing that it's not that bad as I only use the kitchen and the living room. Karen's old room lies empty; it is open for guests that never come and David's room, that door has been closed since he left us. That's the way Lilly wanted it and even towards the end she couldn't bring herself to go in there. God knows what a fright it must be with spider webs and mildew? She closed that door the day he left us, and she swore she would never go in there again and I suppose I just agreed with her and I have always kept my word. I am busy cooking two rashers, checking the dates, frying an egg but it breaks in the middle. I go to lift it off the pan carefully – it may be broken but it tastes good. I make sure my tea is piping hot – it is soothing and I am relieved, my headache subsides at last, the spinning in my head ends, so does the relent-less sound of Sean Cassidy's voice; it worries me no end his voice lives in my brain, calling to me whenever it chooses.

Those days we sat around the fire in Sean Cassidy's house – funny thing as even then I used to remove myself, imagining that I was a stranger outside listening to the music sift through the glow of the tiny window. I thought of the abandoned lonely stranger so cold outside and us, so warm, so safe within the mellow music. Sean Cassidy accompanied softly on the piano; he had such a gentle touch. We might go a shot of Powers or a bottle of stout but the highlight was Irene's tea and cake, which she served around eleven. Lilly thought it a delight and even I found Irene's home baking heavenly. Later on the way home we might pass a stranger lurking down near the gaps. I would go out of my way to say goodnight; sometimes they replied, sometimes they didn't. It was a regular walk for Lilly and me and we even walked it in the snow, slipping and sliding, we holding on for dear life to the garden railings. The kids had made slides along the footpaths during the day but at night they were dark and lethal. It wasn't a long journey, just a half hour or so, but if it snowed it took us a good hour.

Sean Cassidy's sweet voice always in my head, it is like he plays the soundtrack to the movie of my life. I contemplate what I must do now – Anna not coming has thrown cold water on my plans; my whole day is disrupted. I need to go to the post office to post on letters to Karen; they are lying on the bottom shelf of the hall table for months. Each week

I make myself a promise and each week I break it. One of the letters has a coffee stain on it as I just deposited it on the kitchen table – I made amends, putting it away with the three older letters. I guessed they were from the bank; I wonder why the banks write to people so much. Putting the letters in a cloth Dunnes Stores bag (Anna has a heap of them – she hides them in the cupboard under the sink).

I put on my overcoat.

When I go out the day has changed. The wind has picked up – it ruffles the leaves, hassling them till they scatter in all directions. The cars turning into the street have their lights on; the white glow captures the weakness of these redundant torches. The rain clouds come westerly from Rochestown Avenue and some women passing by the Noggin Inn are fiddling with umbrellas. A bus passes noisily. It is empty save for an old lady who stares out the window; she is deep in thought. I make the post office before it shuts. The girl is fresh-faced and friendly, but her colleague is mutton dressed as lamb she has the hair of a teenager yet her face is middle-aged. The girl takes my post; the mutton-dressed-as-lamb woman asks me how Karen is. I say that she is doing really well and I suddenly realise that I always say that and I wonder why as it isn't true. I am glad to hit the damp air once again with the street looking the same as always but me, I feel different somehow. The rain lashes the footpaths erroneously, sending wading ripples across the gutter, it tries and it fails, mocking me and my confused memory.

And I meet Mrs O'Malley from down the gaps. She is buying a stamp. She is sorry to meet me, not that there is any animosity between us, more she didn't want to make idle conversation. I ask her how her husband is. She deflects by talking about the rain, telling me it's down for the week. Then I ask her how her daughter is; she engages with me as she has to now and she turns to me, all hassled, and I see that her lips are dry, all cracked from salt. I think that she is still good-looking save for she chooses to tie her hair back so severe. Her eyes have lost the sparkle of youth and middle age has taken a shining cloth to her skin. She tells me that her Lucy has taken off with a stranger, gone to England against all advice. Father Quigley couldn't persuade her to stay. It's not right, she tells me, a girl of twenty-one going away with an older man like that. Then, while examining her own words, she asks how Karen is and I say she is fine and doing well but I stop for a second and change it to doing as well as expected, on which she interrogates me with a 'Why?' Then she settles for, 'Sure, God love her, after everything.' I pounce, replying, of course, it takes everyone time to settle. She is right about the rain; it falls in buckets. She goes running to the chemist, then shouts back asking how Lilly is. I say she is great, doing her best, life goes on; Lilly loves life you know! Great to hear it, she adds, and I agree with her. I watch the rain drain into the collar of her coat and away she goes.

Leaving her I want to get a mass card signed by Father Quigley. I wonder will Mrs Hughes answer the door. She is so rude and protective. I decide that if he isn't there I can get Father Morris to sign it. The rain is wetting the rim of my hat and getting my head wet; I pass the empty factories and I see the girls leaving hurriedly – they wear blue work coats with no protection from the elements and the rain searches the pores of their skin; they are in good spirits as the day is half done and food awaits. In the distance I hear the thump of machinery. Silent factories as Stroud Reilly comes alive and behind me the girls run for shelter. The Rayon Mills is even quieter; the silence holds all so I am steeped in this common plot. The Noggin has industry.

Mrs Hughes answers the door. I notice a clearing coming from the east. White cloud divides us – it spreads over the new school that was once just the church field – she tells me Father Quigley is in but that he is very busy, I will have to come back later. She is adamant; I can see her eyes bulge beyond her thick-rimmed glasses. She breathes fast, having just run down the stairs. I plead for mercy, telling her I won't be out for at least a week on doctor's orders, what with Flu and all. I know that she recognises me from the choir; but she doesn't want to say so or give it credence; in her world there are no favourites, only rules.

Father Quigley steps out into the hall.

He calls me John and Mrs Hughes steps back to allow him see the whole of me. I laugh, telling him I need a mass card signed for poor old Gerry Brown. The priest beckons me into his study. Mrs Hughes is irked but she accepts that Father Quigley is her superior so she moves on up the stairs. The study is chaotic, with papers piled untidily on the huge table; the priest laments the passing of Gerry Brown, says it is so sad to leave such a young family. The oldest girl has recently joined the choir. 'Kidneys,' he tells me.

I agree as Gerry worked for years on the buses and I was the inspector on his route. We got along – Gerry was a gentleman. Sometimes we would meet in the Victor Hotel for a pint and a chat and Gerry was always generous, even within the rat-like confines of workplace gossip; he was never cynical. Now he was gone, leaving a widow two daughters and a son. Father Quigley speaks fondly of Gerry but he doesn't know him, I can tell; he only knew the parishioners that joined the choir – everyone else was a stranger. He tells me that Gerry Brown's wife wants a mass said in the house, and the difficulty with that is to find a suitable day.

I soon realise how old the parish priest is when his hand shakes as he signs with his fountain pen. When I leave he comes to the door to wave goodbye. I see him as old, and yet he was once so young when waving goodbye many years ago. I continue on, passing the technical school and then back through the gaps, where the stranger still lurks and Lilly is sliding on the ice.

Rain eases, the wind blows from the rear as I pass the houses of several former choir members. Sean Cassidy serenades me with a soft melody. At once I am by his fire; he plays the softest music, his fingers massaging the piano keys, his young son singing 'Where Is Love?' from Oliver, then he's packed off to bed with his brothers and sisters. Sean Cassidy increasing the tempo as the night wore on; he treated us all to the great Richard Tauber. 'You Are My Heart's Delight' followed by 'Love's Old Sweet Song' (just a song at twilight): it was like listening to Tauber himself – and on those snowy journeys through the gaps Lilly hummed the latter, always ending with a comment on Sean Cassidy's beautiful voice.

I am toying with the idea of warming up with a whiskey in the Noggin Inn. I change my mind when I see Don Butler limp across the car park. Don Butler isn't a fellow I want to meet. He is my neighbour three doors up. He has a spread of kids. God knows where they all are now. I know that two of them *are dead and three have done time in prison. The wife is still alive, it is baffling as to how, as Don Butler is as hard and ignorant as they come. No, I don't want to meet him this day. He would corner me, spitting randomly, offering his condolences on Lilly, then speaking in hush tones about David. I go home.*

The street is getting dark; the streetlamps are lit down the far end. I know soon they will light this end also. The lamp outside my house will illuminate the garden and shine right through the front room.

This is where I stand forever looking out, listening to his music, the place that I share with Lilly. She reads her trashy novels by the fireplace, yes, it is here too the stranger sees the soft glow of the lamp, he sees only peace and contentment. I look out at him endlessly from my side, wondering what it is he feels about me now. I go to the cabinet in the kitchen to visit my bottle of Jameson, a gift from Karen last Christmas. To be honest I was surprised she chose whiskey; she said it was good for me, it was a wintery gift, wintery indeed as the night falls upon me for a moment I think of her unhappy marriage. Like I always do I dismiss it; what can I do about this, nothing. The whiskey tastes hot – it burns my throat, then it goes inexplicably cold. I am staring out the window again and the stranger passes, goes up and down the pavement in different guises; he can be a man one minute or a woman or a child the next. I should have never got him the job. He was working with men; he was only twenty years old; he was working on an engine in the depot when the mechanic dropped a spanner. There were three of them all looking into the dirt at the grit, the pistons, the sump. David went to retrieve the spanner when the jack slipped and the engine came down on his head. There was nothing left. He was killed instantly.

The hordes of condolences overwhelmed Lilly and me but he was gone. He left us that day and the truth is I never did know quite what to say to my wife about her son or to my daughter about her brother. I watch the stranger pass; cleverly, he pretends not to look at me; I want to go closer to the window and press my face against the cold glass but I don't as the cold makes me cry. I hear the music once again. Sean Cassidy sings Mario Lanza's 'Oh Holy Night'. Why that song? It isn't Christmas, not for a few months yet. Sean Cassidy was as good as Mario Lanza on his day – well, I always felt that he was.

Yes, I remember now it was that last Christmas in this very room. Sean sang that song and Lilly played for him. Irene and the others were spellbound at the rendition. He stood just about where I stand now, by the fire glowing in the grate, the yellow light flickering on his face. It was the greatest rendition I had ever heard and that included recordings of Lanza himself. It was what the music gave to me that was so important as I thought of Karen and David upstairs asleep and I was at one with the world and the universe; they were so safe. That was the night that Father Quigley came and he sang a song about his own place; he came from a small village in Tipperary. The song was nothing but he had a quiver in his voice that wasn't there usually and I saw a soft tear fall from his left eye when he finished. Sean Cassidy said something funny just to lighten the moment. Father Quigley laughed loudly and suddenly his equilibrium returned.

I loved that night just like I have grown to love the Jameson. The more of it I drink, the less cold the world outside becomes. I get this mad urge to light the fire but my head is spinning again. I have no coal in the bucket; this means having to go out to the shed. But the fire is exactly what I need. It is a struggle, the heavy kitchen door, then the chill attacks my throat. The whiskey fortifies me so I am brave. Unbolting the shed, the lock has been broken for months and I fill the steel bucket with the dark, dusty black stones. The weight of it pulls at my groin, all down my right side it is particularly sore. I rest it for a second, just waiting to bolt the shed and pick it up again; the thoughts of more whiskey encourage me. I am sure that a few more shots will cure my aching groin too. And it does, but my fire takes an age to catch. Me left standing in the cold, the draught is cutting into my lower back and I am sure Lilly would have chastened me for standing so close to the door.

In her final years she read many books. Lilly collected big words, which she threw at me from time to time. One day she told me that I was iniquitous when I voiced my disapproval of Karen's proposed marriage, her move to live in Cork. Lilly thought that Tim Cronin was a gentleman and a successful businessman. But I knew man to man what he was and that he eyed a younger woman to give him offspring; after that he would continue on with his roguish rugby humour and his college-boy affections. Karen complains that he is out all of the time and some nights he doesn't come home at all. She blames herself when he raises his fists, saying things like it was her own fault as he came home from work tired and frustrated. I can't understand what all the pressure is, after all he inherited Daddy's car business and I guess he just sits around in an office all day.

The fire sparks and Lilly tells me to pull the curtains to let the stranger wander into the night. When she was really ill she spoke of David. It was strange because for so many years she barely said his name: such was our existence, to eat and drink, to live and survive in denial. But she spoke of him and it was very simple. She said that she was looking forward to seeing him again.

I pull the curtains. I spit at the stranger. The streetlight makes a glow on the curtain; it looks like it is burned in one rounded spot. I take its heat, the whiskey is almost gone. I fret, just enough left for two glasses. I hear Lilly give out. She tells me not to be drinking so much, that the drink won't change anything. I reply, Well, at least it will numb the pain; but it doesn't really, it only numbs me momentarily. I am giddy now.

I leave my fire; I need to use the toilet. Climbing the short stairs to the landing I see Karen's room and our room, the lonely closed door of David's room. I use the toilet; when I return I am thinking of him. From the time he learned to walk to all the different phases of school, sport, his communion and confirmation. I remember watching him play ball with the kids out on the street and for some daft reason the way he held Karen's hand when she took him to the sweet shop down at Honeypark.

Staying on the landing, I am mad; I am mad at myself, somehow I am mad at Lilly. Why not go into his room? Why not see the place where he lived and slept all of those years? I climb the next three steps, turning the handle on his door, it opens easily and to my surprise there is no musty smell. I turn on the light; everything dazzles white; the fly window is ajar as it was the way he left it.

I feel the wind seeping through, fanning my face. His pillows propped up under a blanket and his sheets neatly turned back over the bedspread. Two magazines lay flat on his bedside locker, one about motor bikes, the other was a holiday travel mag – this one had faded slightly, the ink was disappearing; beside them a trashy detective yarn by Mickey Spillane. The wardrobe doors are ajar; the chest of drawers closed fast with some live fur balls gathering in the crevices on the carpet.

Under the mirror there is a photograph taken not long before he left us. He stares at me, his hair combed away from his eyes so neatly, yes, I remember that smirk. David found the world to be a very funny place. I laugh along with him. I find myself laughing loudly and then I walk quickly to the wardrobe, yanking the door open, expecting to find some stranger lurking. All his clothes, his leather jacket, his three pairs of denim jeans. Beside these are his good clothes: his slacks and his sports jacket and below that two pairs of shoes, one leather, one suede. He had four pairs of runners, all neatly stacked on top of each other. I pull out the drawers with his underwear and tee shirts all neatly folded but dust has fouled the edges of the ones at the top.

This room that is dead is somehow coming alive, over

on the window sill there is a photo of his girlfriend, Teresa Brogan. She is married since. I think she has five children. She was a pretty thing even if given to putting on weight. I know that he loved her because he spoke about her so much; he always said that she made him laugh. I know I liked that as I must have said it to Lilly a thousand times until she got fed up with me and started to say it for me, before I could get my words out. I look back once before I close the door and I vow to never go back into that room again.

I stand on the landing in the stillness; I can hear Lilly sing as she cleans, as she changes the sheets. I call out to her and she calls back joyously, telling me that she is in David's room.

You are my heart's delight,
And where you are, I long to be
You make my darkness bright,
When like a star you shine on me
Shine, then, my whole life through
Your life divine bids me hope anew
That dreams of mine may at last come true
And I shall hear you whisper,
'I love you.'

In dreams when night is falling
I seem to hear you calling
For you have cast a net around me
And 'neath a magic spell hath bound me
Yours, yours alone
How wondrous fair is your beautiful hair
Bright as a summer sky

Nogginers

is the night in your eyes
Soft as a sparkling star
is the warmth of my love.

You are my heart's delight,
And where you are, I long to be
You make my darkness bright,
When like a star you shine on me
Shine, then, my whole life through
Your life divine bids me hope anew
That dreams of mine may at last come true
And I shall hear you whisper,
'I love you.'

Betty Drew

1973

It is near the end now. What of it? Both Elizabeth and George have gone. Young George and Martina are still around. Young George is strong with Jenny Toner and that looks like being a great marriage. Martina will stay. She will never marry. I fear for her; she will end up like me. They have a dreadful word they use for people like me – a spinster – what a horrible word; it is akin to being called monster, or dumpster. Maybe it should be the name of a new province. We could have Munster, Ulster, Leinster, and Spinster and we could do away with Connacht altogether.

How Elizabeth laughed when I said that to her. 'Go away,' she said, 'go away with you, Betty.' She looked at me over the kitchen table, saying, 'Yah never know, sister, maybe one of the Breslin brothers will take a shine to you, ask you out.'

I replied smartly, 'I don't go for bald men, Elizabeth, their heads are too shiny, and those Breslins have heads on them like tortoises peeping out from under their shells.'

Elizabeth died laughing; her face contorting, she threw it forward, towering over the surface of the table. I thought she was going to lose her nose in a mug for a second. I pulled the plates and mugs away from her.

'Maybe Mrs Edge will fix you up?' She could barely speak such was her excitement.

'A spinster I am, a spinster I will stay no doubt.'

I watched her expression change, so taken was she by the seriousness of my statement. I tried to smile in an effort to lighten things. Elizabeth was having none of it.

'Mammy would be very sad for you, Betty.'

She was back to sitting up straight now.

'Mammy always said to Daddy that she had high hopes for you, you were the dark horse.' Elizabeth stopped talking; she looked at me intently. It was like she was expecting another great outburst from me and when there was none coming, she said softly, 'Marriage isn't everything, you know?'

I wanted to say, 'Yes, I know, because every time this conversation comes up you say the same bloody thing at one point or another, whatever it means, Elizabeth. Marriage isn't everything, what does that actually mean? To me marriage means everything. I am not married, so I sleep alone, I eat many meals alone and Goddamn it I dream alone. I never get the comfort of a man, just feel his warm body on top of me. Don't, Elizabeth, don't tell me that marriage isn't everything, you that has a husband and two children.'

Poor Elizabeth. She was always so good to me, right the way through, always so kind and decent and it wasn't that she had to look out for me, mind, no not at all. If anything I should have looked out for her! I was two years older.

The good thing about cancer is that sometimes it can manifest itself in your body and then riddle it with disease soes you will be dead in no time. That is what happened to Elizabeth. There she was, hale and hearty, sitting at the kitchen table eating buns, and she was the picture of health. Yes, she was giving out about George, about the chores he did for Mrs Edge, how she was stealing his time, wearing him out.

It was a cold Saturday afternoon, one of those semi-dark days when the world doesn't light up properly. I wanted to tell her that George was doing more than chores for Mrs Edge but I hadn't the heart as Elizabeth had a propensity to deal with everything innocently. She just hadn't got that battle-hardened sense of cynicism that I had. I blamed my illness for that – well, my illness and some other things.

A month later she was dead, yet it was on another dreary kitchen Saturday that she said, 'They're very worried about the blood. He says the tests will tell us more. I don't like him, Betty, he reminds me of yer man Curtis down the road or you know yer man the politician Healy with the big eyebrows. I get the willies, it's like his eyes are hidin under those big bushes.'

'Stop now, girl,' I said.

'Isn't it a wonder what they can do these days with their

tests and the like? I'd swear you have a kidney stone. I would guess yer appendix, save I was there when they burst.'

'A nightmare,' Elizabeth held my gaze, her eyes soaking.

'He warned me. He said it might be cancer, that diagnosis won't be good, Betty!'

'What did George say?'

'He said nuthin!'

'Well you would think he'd say somethin?'

'Suppose he did, kind of – he said it was probably nuthin, just to go ahead and get my tests done.'

'Break yer heart, George, why don't you?'

'Maybe he was a bit shocked, he was just sitting on the bed pulling up his trousers. He was off to work, they're fierce busy in there.'

'Dunno,' I said. 'They're complaining when there are no ships, and complaining more when the docks are full.'

'That's the nature of it,' Elizabeth said, stretching her left hand across the table for me to take ahold of it.

Elizabeth attributed everything to nature – she often used that term, to her it was the perfect excuse for everything. And as nature would have it, she had stomach cancer and there was nothing they could do. I tried my best to console her. Young George did his best to perk her up. He was saying stuff about miracle cures, stuff he had read in some new book that was all the rage. Martina didn't say much, yet for those three weeks she barely left her mother's side. Sitting with her drinking tea and embracing her for no apparent reason before wiping the tears from her mother's face. We must have drunk gallons of tea, one pot after another.

Near the end George stayed home. He watched television in the living room but he didn't say much as he wasn't a very talkative man. Yet he was more civil than usual and he even spoke softly to Elizabeth during meals. Usually he was a terror when at the table and he invariably picked on me just to irk his wife. But now he was soft and quiet and attentive. When Martina mentioned Mrs Edge, he didn't comment, he just let his daughter rant on about the woman; he acting like she was a complete stranger. I watched him finish his bacon and cabbage, his thin face was only handsome because his eyes sparkled but the rest of him was rugged, his nose was long and pointed but those eyes sucked you in though and in fairness to him it was enough to win a woman over.

'What time is the boy home?' he asked his wife.

'Whatever time they let him off,' she replied weakly.

''Tis no job for a boy, selling televisions, no future in televisions – it will be like the films, advance itself to death.'

Elizabeth looked at her husband mournfully, then she glanced kindly at Martina and me before saying, 'It is only a start-up job, sure, he's gaining experience.'

Her husband was satisfied that he eaten enough; he placed his knife and fork ritually across the plate.

'I told him about the ships but he had no interest. He said he would be seasick. The money is ten times better, sure he might meet a man or two?'

'Mammy's tired,' Martina said. I shuddered as father and daughter didn't see eye to eye, they rarely communicated outside of the normal pleasantries.

'You're right, George,' Elizabeth said. 'It is no job selling televisions. I will chat to him and maybe he will have another think about it?'

'It's too late!'

Elizabeth winced as he lifted his plate and then walked past her and dropped it into the sink full of suds. 'I might dig up the flower beds, it's that time of year.' He was suddenly soft once again so I started to relax. 'We could have a good summer,' he said. 'After all the rain we had; they say it will be good anyway.' He was gone out the back; the cold from the open kitchen door replaced him momentarily until he closed it from the outside.

'More tea,' Martina said.

'I can't,' her mother replied, 'I am teed out,' but I had one just to please Martina.

Later, when young George arrived home, I gave him his dinner in the kitchen. He was subdued when he normally would have been eager and full of chat. Martina was in the sitting room reading whilst her father had gone out but didn't say where he was going. Elizabeth was in the living room by the fire; she had started watching television, but she was soon asleep.

'What are you up to?' I teased.

'Jenny's ma wants me to hang some wallpaper and I don't want to do it but Jenny says I better, just to get in with the oul wan like. She's mad keen on me doing it. I swear, Betty, it's like her whole life depends on it, a few rolls of wallpaper, Jesus.' I watched him eat his food, he was ferocious yet in fairness he was tidy enough, he chewed slowly and he didn't stuff himself, he just ate loads but neatly.

'The poor woman is demented,' I said. 'Sure Henry is much older than her and he hasn't any strength these days.'

'I know,' young George said, 'but he is hell of a nice fella, he loves a chat; he's mad into United, everythin is United this and United that.'

'Surprised he takes to you so, George, and you an Everton man.'

'Nah, he doesn't mind at all; he sits all evening by the fire talkin football. He talks to me about Everton but then he switches back to United.'

'Not easy for him, though, he must be ten years older than her?'

George, finishing his food, said, 'He is a good twelve years older, you know he is always saying how he should have stayed a bachelor, he says the marriage killed him. I swear he tells me that!'

'That's a terrible thing to say about his wife,' I said.

'That's what he says but he's probably only messin!'

There was something about George that evening, with his chained exuberance and his nervous youthfulness. I could see his father in him, but it was the wonderful traces of Elizabeth that made his face rounder even more handsome than his father. He had her smile too, which endeared him to me and for all that I loved Martina, he was definitely my favourite. He was the light of my life.

I never cared for the Toners but Jenny's a nice girl, mind, she is good-hearted and very pure in a decent Catholic way. Her mother is a tyrant, though, and as common as muck, yet the father comes from a better family. My mother knew his mother; they worked together in the Sweep, but that was years ago. Elizabeth always wondered how they got one of the corner sites around the block. Mr Toner was a dental technician but he never really worked at that. He spent years in the gas company and then he had a taxi plate for a while. He hasn't worked for years and she does a bit of cleaning. Jimmy Hollywood knew old Toner from the football club. He did say that he liked him, however I always felt he was holding something back. What I dunno, all I knew was that old Toner was as cute as they come. Elizabeth in her naivety didn't realise that she never knew Mr Toner had lots of contacts in the Corporation when the houses came to be allocated.

Jimmy Hollywood used call to see Elizabeth. There was nothing going on, mind. My mother and father went to bed and left us sitting up listening to records in the living room. Jimmy lived in old Dun Leary; his father was dead and his mother in a home, she was incapacitated with Motor Neurone disease. He had one younger sister who, in fairness, he cared for diligently, much to the liking of all who knew him. He was a tall, skinny, gregarious chap with a steel chin leading to strong nose, which sort of rounded him off. He liked to sit on my father's armchair when he departed for bed. It was close to the fire so he stretched his long legs out over the hearth.

Elizabeth, uninterested, yawned. 'Time to go home, Jimmy,' she said blandly.

'Not a bit of it, sure as the fella said we are only starting,' he said gaily.

'Put on another record,' I encouraged him but Elizabeth said, 'One more now, and keep it low.' She yawned again.

Jimmy put on Elvis Presley, the sound was too low to enjoy it but to annoy Elizabeth he moved his arms rapidly just like the top of his body was detached, he flailing his arms about like he was on the dance floor.

'I'm going to bed,' Elizabeth announced, 'yah can see yourself out, Jimmy. Well for Betty to want to rave; she doesn't have to work in the morning.'

Jimmy just smiled at Elizabeth. She left through the living room door. But he was quiet when she was gone, he was just staring into the fire like he was lost.

'Will I play that again?' I said, 'I can turn it up if you want.'

'Nah, don't bother,' he said, 'we might wake them upstairs.'

'Are you alright, Jimmy?'

'I am. I was jus hopin Elizabeth might stay up a bit – that's all; no use in me mopin on about it, is there?'

'She's tired,' I said. 'She gets like that when she's tired.'

'I best be going so.'

When he stood I could see how tall and bandy he was. 'You can stay if yah want, Jimmy, I can do us some toast on the fire.'

'Nah I will head on, Betty, best let you go to yer bed.' He patted me on the head and he left.

That night and for many more nights to come I couldn't sleep. It was like a mist descended on me and for a while I couldn't take to my younger sister at all. Here she was with a handsome man at her beck and call, yet it didn't seem to disturb her, not a bloody inch. She was always petulant with him or blatantly flirting so, leading him on before then rebuking him when he got too close.

It got to the stage where I was determined to challenge her, confront her with all the facts of her lousy behaviour. And then I thought, she will find me out. For weeks I couldn't think of another thing. Jimmy Hollywood was in my head night and day and it was getting worse as I began to imagine he was in bed with me.

As I drifted off to sleep there he was all fine and him with his athletic body cosying up to me. His hands rubbing my hips and thighs, waiting patiently, he slips his fingers, they warmly sinking into the crevice between my legs. I stopped to listen to see if Elizabeth was awake. I could hear her soft breathing; suddenly she turned to face the wall and this followed by silence. Jimmy began again, this time stroking me, his circular movement making me dance. I sang for him, horrifyingly, it was so loud that Elizabeth shot up in her bed, 'Are you alright, Betty?' But I was alright.

'I was havin a dream; go back asleep.' Elizabeth groaned and fainted back into oblivion. I secretly hugged Jimmy till I fell asleep. In the morning when I woke he was gone but, alarmingly, the sheet underneath me was damp. I started planning to get rid of it. How could I get it cleaned? If I put it in the wash basket, will it be found? I got a brainwave. I will throw Elizabeth's sheets in with it, then nobody can tell. It could be one or it could be the other, oh yes, that was the only sensible thing to do.

The day he announced that he was going to Cork to live flattened me. I nearly lost my reason. For ages I had been planning to tell him how I felt; I was thrilled when Elizabeth met George Drew, naturally I gathered the courage to out my feelings. George was so sweet on Elizabeth; conveniently, his people were hard-working and respectable. George's father collected money for the Fine Gael party and he came calling by selling raffle tickets – sometimes George accompanied him, but he came on his own when his father got ill and he engaged Elizabeth in flirtatious exchanges at the front door. So this was my time to speak out as she was smitten with him, at last Jimmy Hollywood would be all mine. But then he made his announcement; to make matters worse he didn't even say it to me like in private. No, he just marched in and said it to my parents, I can see him now as clear as day warming his backside by the fire.

'We are going to Cork to live with my aunt. She is a widow, you know? For years; her husband died when the children were very young. She is lonely on her own these days, she has a big house in Douglas.'

My father quizzed him about the detail, and my mother unusually flopped into the armchair.

'It's all arranged – it will be a big move but sure as the fella said we will get on with it!'

I tried to catch his eye as he spoke, like I wanted him to see the tears manufacturing; my eyes, they were now just desolate wet abandoned tear factories. But he held his gaze over me; it was like he was seeking my parents' approval above all else. He turned and he was gone, passing Elizabeth and George at the front door, and I followed till I lost sight of him at the gate.

'What's wrong with you, Betty?' Elizabeth said. Uncomfortably, she acted like she was in awe of George, and she didn't want me to make a show.

'Nothing!' I said, not wanting to make a fuss or to tell her that Jimmy was leaving for good.

The doctor said it was down to Jimmy Hollywood, he connived with me, agreeing that it was Jimmy who broke my heart. But my heart was broken a long time before him. He wrote to me once; I ran up the stairs to my room and I sat on the bed panting. I eased the envelope open before I read the letter over and over, then I read it again looking for hidden clues. Did he miss me even in a casual way?

He was going on about how wonderful his aunt was, how comfortable their lives were now in the big house. It was set back from the road with a gravel drive and an old oak tree that shaded all. His sister loved it – she loved her bedroom that was huge in comparison to her old one; Jimmy was delighted he got a job in the builders' providers out the Kinsale Road – the money wasn't great but the craic was mighty and all in all you would never find a better set of fellas. I could have read it a thousand times but it was useless as there was no mention of missing me or even Elizabeth for that matter.

The letters stopped suddenly after his mother passed away in the nursing home; I dunno maybe he felt her death closed all of his ties with us and Dun Laoghaire.

So as I got low I realised that all Jimmy Hollywood did was break a heart that was already cracked and glued together with jelly. It happens when a little girl looks in the mirror and realises that she is different. I had to drag my left foot like there was big stone tied to it, that was bad enough, of course; hideously, I was plain to go with it and there is no curing that. Elizabeth was perfect: her perfection entitled her to a happiness that I could never aspire to nor would I ever deserve.

I stayed five years on and off in the hospital, sadly during this time both my parents died. They went within three months of each other, my perfect parents with the respectable family that was now no longer, we were ripped apart by nature. My life was interrupted by my polio and I suppose my breakdown just completely ruined all. It was Elizabeth who came to fetch me. She brought me into the bosom of her family, allowing me to hide within the respectability they automatically created. The day I arrived I was struck by this numinous aura of sameness and good, to be honest it sucked me in and gave me warmth and reason for the first time in my life. To make matters perfect the neighbours assimilated me without question to the Drews, and I became known as Betty Drew, even though I was never a Drew nor could I ever be.

Young George got married a year to the day after Elizabeth died. It was a dull affair as weddings go. The bride was dressed elegantly. She looked far more beautiful than, of course, she actually was, testament to the wonders of modern makeup. George was dashing; he was doing his best to be cheerful and bright, unfortunately I guess Elizabeth was still haunting us all. So despite the gay colours and the charade the whole occasion had a solemn attachment that was ner do well to a proper celebration.

Martina wore a fine dress that I helped her pick out – it was light blue with a floral pattern propping up the breast line. I liked that dress as it highlighted how tall she was whilst stealing her plump bits and somehow I felt it made her face shine. I was watching George Sr; I was still expecting to see him rub Mrs Edge on the shoulder stealthily. He did use his hand to embrace the lady beside him, yet it wasn't Mrs Edge. Meet Maureen, never found out her surname, such embarrassment as George Sr caused consternation when he turned up accompanied by a woman none of us had ever seen or heard of before. She was extra thin, yet her face was much fuller despite that. She had long, slender hands that sort of spider-legged through the air to greet you. I didn't take to her at all as I thought she had cold brown eyes with way too much blue mascara painted round them.

She spoke nervously, her voice squeaking like a mouse when George Sr introduced us but miraculously she greeted each of us in turn like she had known us intimately all of our lives. George Sr was brazen about her – he didn't flinch when young George took him to one side in an effort to get some clarity as to who this woman was.

Mrs Edge had said she wouldn't come to the wedding at all on account of Maureen, whom she had only found out about at the eleventh hour when George Sr had phoned her. However, in the end she said she relented on account of young George and Martina, stating how it would be so unfair on them if she didn't turn up, and her a family friend for all of these years.

She had given me a somewhat different account a day earlier when she wound back the clock, calling unexpectedly that afternoon. Mrs Edge was a widow; her poor husband had died in an accident not long after she was married. I always thought that she had that stolen look. Life had stolen something from her and she just made do as best she could, and maybe she occupied her mind greatly with her obsession on stealing things back from the world. She dressed elegantly, her clothes clinging to her voluptuous figure, allowing her breasts to swing pendulum-like when she walked. She carried herself forward through the strength of her cheekbones protecting the sheer magnetism of her eyes. I brought her to the kitchen only because that's where Elizabeth always brought her; I made her tea and gave her a bun that was losing its freshness. She took it gleefully, eating it quickly, the crumbs sprinkling on her saucer like fluttering snow.

'I can't believe it, Betty, he just came out with it without a bye or leave; I mean what was I supposed to say?'

I wanted to say that he had recently buried my sister, his wife, and what the hell was going on? I didn't. I just said sympathetically, 'Men are funny creatures, you wouldn't know what's got into him.'

'I know – and we have been friends for so long – so many years, Betty.'

Friends. Some friend you were, I wanted to say; he was married to your friend, my sister, and you always entertaining him down in that little love nest by the people park. But I didn't say that, either. I just said, 'Easy now.'

Mrs Edge was sobbing uncontrollably. I went to the counter to get her a paper tissue and she accepted it gratefully, wiping her eyes and then blowing her nose loudly.

'I am so sorry, Betty, putting this on you and poor Elizabeth barely settled in her grave.'

'It's not a worry; it is such a shame she is gone.'

'You know he has been with her a least a year, that is what gets to me, you know, calling by to see me, and he was in with her behind my back.' She started to splutter again, this time she used the same tissue to stem the flow of tears. 'Every time I think of it!'

I wanted to scream like every time I think of the two of you messing about behind my poor sister's back but again I stayed quiet. Mrs Edge, finally noting my discomfort, said, 'You must hate me, Betty, all of you must hate me really. I suppose I shouldn't show up at the wedding now, it wouldn't be fair. Like I always felt some legitimacy, you know, George said he loved me; he always told me that he loved me. He said ...' Mrs Edge hesitated.

I, frustrated, snarled, 'What did George say?'

'Nothing much, Betty, just that his marriage to Elizabeth was over; he said he stayed for the children to support the family. It was gone like – he didn't get anything from it.' She stopped to see how I took to her words. Whatever reaction I gave her, she got to her feet quickly, she was making to go.

'We always knew, all of us, even Elizabeth,' I said, 'but she chose to ignore it, that was her way, she didn't really do confrontation, not with George anyhow. I think she left all her feistiness in a bin somewhere when she first met him.'

'You knew?' Mrs Edge was shocked. 'Did he tell you?'

'No,' I said, 'he did not, but we knew just the same.'

She was quiet at the wedding, polite to those who engaged with her, but I saw the daggers she fired across the room aimed at George Sr and Maureen, who embraced each other occasionally like true lovebirds. But like a lot of things in the world it didn't last. Maureen soon succumbed to the wonderful charms of another, whilst George Sr unsuccessfully tried to reignite his flame with Mrs Edge, but in fairness to the woman she had moved on. But he didn't, he became sullener and isolated. He didn't go the pub for a pint anymore and everything now was just bed to work. He ate his meals quietly, engaging with nobody, not even his daughter, whom he would answer with grumpy sighs and unintelligible utterances till she gave up and didn't attempt to speak to him anymore. I watched him though. I listened for sounds from his bedroom. I held his sweaty shirts over my face before I put on a wash. The manly odour from his skin after a tired day at work, all of this, along with gazing at his wonderful skin sparkle when he shaved the dead hair from his chin. I wanted him now and I was lying in wait for him.

Memories of Jimmy Hollywood, but it was George Sr who entered my bed. He warmed me between my legs, suddenly I felt the power of his manliness on top of me, he bit into my neck till I cried out unashamedly only for Martina to knock at my bedroom door and cry out.

'Yes, I am alright, Martina,' I shouted back.

George Sr drowned in an accident down the docks. It wasn't a suicide, the guards made sure to tell us that. Evidently he fell through a rotted plank of wood on the gangway of some Polish ship when he was carrying a case of Polish vodka, a reward for a negative search, no doubt.

Me, I took to the stuff then. The mighty vodka – sometimes I mixed it with orange or coke but most times I drank it neat. Today I climbed the step ladder after drinking far too much of the stuff, alarmingly this is the third time this has happened this year. I wasn't trying to hang myself or anything daft like that, no, but I have taken to cleaning the light shade at the top of the landing. It is so high and decorative, yet it is always out of my reach, but I am afraid I slipped, so I toppled over and down the stairs. I hit my head, now the blood is streaming across the tiles. I have broken my right leg I am sure. I am done. But what of it, sure they are all gone now, one by one they fell. Martina will come home and find me gone too but she will be alright as young George will call by with the children on Sundays. She just dotes over them. I am done, as they say, God is good, it makes me laugh that, I can feel the cold it sends ice jets from my arse to my shoulders so maybe I should try to move, after all I carried my foot for years. I have inhuman strength.

Weekly with Mrs Tims

1985

I can remember the sea. That's what I remember most from those days, sitting in the back of a sticky car, the plastic seats burning my calves. And then one of my cousins would spy the sea, a deep blue postcard. I think I owe so much to John Hinde; you do know the factory was up in Cabinteely just by the village? Yes, John Hinde created the perfect world.

My aunt driving this escort station wagon; it was her pride and joy, her pride anyhow. We raced on to the deep blue postcard and her escort was good over the rough terrain. Getting the swim gear out of the boot, I used to imagine it as a hearse, a big black hearse. The sand was burning the soles of my feet, and when you stepped onto one of those prickly straw-like things they splintered up to the heart. Us day-trippers road sign counters through the Glen of the Downs, and onto Ashford. Road signs we called burnies as they resembled upturned cigarettes smouldering by the roadside, they were lighted butts awaiting stubbing.

Mrs Tims says, 'So why do you think about this?'

'Why not?'

'I am just trying to see if it has any significance.'

'I dunno, maybe it does maybe it doesn't.'

'You tell me!'

'It might have had no significance, maybe? I am middle-aged balding now; it has lots of significance.'

'Perhaps.'

'I dunno!'

'Did you like your cousins?'

'I did – when we were kids. I did – but we grew differently – I guess there was lots to like about them. I didn't like the climb over the dunes; it really gets the back of your legs, you know sometimes you could hardly lift your feet with the depth of the sand. They always brought creamed chocolate éclairs, now there is a thing.'

'Come on now? I mean éclairs are hardly lavish.'

'Nah, you're right – those days were just ebullient, there is no explanation, they just were. You see my cousins could all swim really good; I think they got regular lessons. I was afraid of the water like I might just splash around the edge. Sitting up to my waist, the water crystal-clear, wetting me, and splashing up to my chest. I was feeling really brave. My cousins could dive in from the side of damaged piers. Everything was a race just to see how quickly they could run round in a circle, do it all again. Sometimes I wondered what they saw when they hit the water with their heads submerged, whatever it was they never told me. I guess it couldn't have been much.'

'Did you want to see?'

'Wouldn't you?'

'I dunno – you tell me.'

'I think you would, Mrs Tims. I think you definitely would.'

'Maybe – but perhaps you don't know me that well?'

'Don't think they saw that much – no more than me sitting by the shore – all that cold water seeping into me. It's funny, isn't it, how the water is so cold at first and then it gets kinda warm?'

'The body just gets used to it, I suppose.'

'Did you ever notice how time stays still on a beach – yeah like it's still moving but it's only movin elsewhere, but everythin around you stays kinda static – did you ever feel that, Mrs Tims, or do you think it might just be me? I reckon it's down to everyone just havin a good time like it's different if yah see folk walkin the main street of the town, isn't it? Everyone on the beach is walkin around half-naked getting wet, then getting dry, us worshippin the sun is that it? Is that why time stands still, because we have returned to sun worshippin?'

Mrs Tims says, 'I dunno – do you think we should worship the sun?'

'Yeah, I do – it's all so much better than this religious crap!'

'Who made the sun?'

'I give up, Mrs Tims, who?'

'Some people say God made the sun!'

'Do they? I suppose when Christians sunbathe, they sort of have the edge then. Their guy made it – methinks they should be soakin it up.'

'Of course people are different on the beach; they go there to have fun – as you say, peel off, catch the rays. They swim and play games, whatever – but why do you get this idea that time stands still?'

'I don't – I just think that it is moving far away; out on the roads, up in the sky – but whilst you're on the beach, it stops, and you are in the only relevant thing in the whole wide world!'

'So your cousins shared the chocolate éclairs then?'

'They did – they were always generous with the éclairs – food was always a big thing to my aunt and my mother – they fed us like we were baby pigs; all gathered around in a circle to feed at the teat but we got egg-and-tomato sandwiches instead, and our éclairs.'

'Why didn't you swim?'

'I was never taught!'

'Most folk learn themselves – well especially back then!'

'My cousins were in a swimming club – they were great swimmers – they had more money than we had!'

'Yes, I know – they could afford chocolate éclairs!'

'That's it.'

'So tell me why you wake up at night – tell me exactly what happens.'

'I just can't move – there is always some presence, like a stranger, at first it all appears numinous but after a while I can sense the malevolence, that dreadful sense of what lurks in the shadows and sometimes they don't just threaten me but other people who are close to me, like my kids, and they are always in a different room, one that I can't get to.'

'So what happens?'

'I freeze, I cannot move a muscle. I am paralysed. My mind is perfect but I am trapped in this powerless body. I am trying to invigorate it, trying so hard to give it life, to give it use again!'

'Frightening!'

'Insane!'

'How often does this happen?'

'I dunno – every now and then!'

It was much better when I was with my own kind, there was always easiness about things. Nah, they were just as special as anyone else; it was more that in the Noggin you didn't have to impress. We were the common birds. I dunno I think I realised that one time my cousins came over to play. All my pals became normalites, what I was used to, they became mundane and common; it was like their entire colour was sucked out. This wasn't my cousins' fault, it was me. I plead guilty to that; gone were the shreds, these bits of black and white, all my movies played themselves out. Flat accents; industrial uniforms; boys washed, well-scrubbed; girls prettified in frilly frocks. One of my own held me over the bathroom chair and she slapped my bare bottom and I was barely four, but I knew, I knew straight away. Yeah, the muck parties where the boys would make muck cakes put the earthworms in; maggots make currents; drifted how this magnified world became the Colorado River. Thinking of Westerns: *How the West Was Won*, Karl Malden, and 'Greensleeves', high on emotion, knowing that some geek would tell you that tune was written by Henry the 8th.

Mrs Tims says, 'So tell me about the waterlogged fields.'

'That was much later.'

'Was it, sorry – so what is it you want to talk about now?'

'Nothing – I'm tired of talking.'

'Do you want to rest?'

'No, I'm not tired like that, just fed up!'

'We have time – that's one thing we have plenty of.'

'That's the problem.'

'What's the problem?'

'Time!'

'Why?'

'It eats us alive, that's why!'

'Same for everyone.'

'That doesn't help – it doesn't make things any better.'

'There is nothing can be done about it – seems like a wasteful obsession.'

'Yeah, I agree – but if you go back to my normalites you will see – how about these boys running up the right of way by Killiney golf course, slapping their arses, riding fake horses?'

'Kids what age?'

'Pick an age – we will say ten and younger.'

'On they run by the caddy master's shack – get it, caddy shack – there he is, good old sinister Jack, "Jack the nigger from Ballybrack," you can't say that anymore, but I just did.'

'Was he coloured?'

'No, no – he either didn't wash or he was just very sallow.'

'Hah ha ha.'

'If he wasn't around we ran onto the course itself – only late in the evening or when it was very quiet – the older lads took refuge in a bunker; the rest of us all charged – riddle riddle grenade grenade – riddle aaaaaaaaah – riddle-grenade – aaaaaaaaaah.'

'Sounds fun.'

'I won – all; the other normalites were clutching their chests, falling this way and that. I won – I clutched my forehead falling backwards; I won!'

'Well done!'

'I won "Who Falls the Best"!'

I sued those memories. I have taken action against time, I wanna go back to the safe house; all of us sleeping all safe and warm. I hear the gentle normal sounds from outside and then sleep descends like dust. No little boy lying awake; no frowns or dressing gowns, no closets; no presses in the hall or me full of air sitting, caterwauling on the stairs, only small panes of glass block me from the world. Is it the same small world; think of all of those lives running parallel, living trains only meet where the lines cross. Was it here that I met my first religious bigot or was it more important to step out and feel the magical snow? I used to think there was a guy who lived in the centre of the earth, winding it all up like a clockwork, the tic-toc man. Very hot – still there are fellas who might do it – then there are fellas who would do anything.

   Oh, for some maggot pie.

Mrs Tims says, 'Do you want to tell me about later on?'
   'Do I?'
   'Thought you might.'
   'No!'
   'Ok!'
   'Dunno!'
   'Maybe we should end then?'
   'Whatever!'
   'You sound angry.'
   'No, I don't get angry – only my throat does.'
   'Your throat?'
   'Yeah, my throat is weak – all my emotions go through my throat.'
      'Hah ha, you are a funny man.'
      'Funny little man, you mean.'

Because existence is burnt smoke, these stolen embers stalking ghosts. Once on this trip to the Sugar Loaf I grew up and I smelt the daisies for the second time. We brought a picnic; two girls came; that in itself was unusual. Imagine planting the frustration weed in the side of a mountain, then imagine watching it grow. Now I take frustration, embrace it like it is life's nectar, so maybe it's the giant marble that spins inside your belly as the internal world spins off of its axis just to couple with rusted nerves and then jangle with worn intestinal belts. I get off among the Wicklow heather, and she is spinning by me, all young and fair. I just wanted to touch her skin, gaze at her lazy frock forever – there is no knowing this as knowledge leads to conceit, and on to boredom with reluctant acceptance.

Mrs Tims says, 'Infatuation.'

'A great word for those without the imagination, to be infatuated!'

'I didn't know you needed imagination.'

'Think about it!'

'Well, do you?'

'Of course you do – this girl could have danced naked in front of the others; they wouldn't have paid a blind bit of notice.'

'Really?'

'Yes!'

'Odd, isn't it?'

'What's odd is that we never got together – but hell, now it makes no difference.'

'Makes no difference – why does it make no difference?'

'Why would it? It never happened. Everything is pretty useless so what fucking difference would it make – like all else, it would have become contemptuous and fractious, so who cares?'

'You do, or you would never bring it up.'

'Yeah?'

'Tell me.'

'She was nothing. There are millions of her in the world but there isn't millions of me, no, there is just me.'

Corpus Christi

1974

Father Morris, his shoulders hunched, he made his face touch the mirror; what would a boy think of that? All that blasphemy, the goo that sticks to the insides of his wet head, deep in there lies a million places and a thousand children with deep-set eyes. It was repugnant to him that some of the kids looked undernourished – this was despite his reservation on the causes of poverty, in essence he now rejoiced in what he had come to call positive discrimination; mainly as it was the plumpness and wellness he might crave. A bit of meat; it is what Joyce might have referred to as 'robust', or just plain rude. He moved to the other side of the mirror as it was cracked down the centre, and he had a fixation with the top quarter, so if he stood on his toes he could see the clarity of his own skin, which failed to please as it kept a jaundiced look, but he didn't mind that as it definitely was better than the porter red blush that dominated the lower quarter.

For a moment he thought about skin, while acknowl-
edging that he had piles of it, his little wafer, dusty layers
piled on brick by brick, then drained by a million holes, he
was water-based and oozing mortar. This is my skin; and
when he moved, his eyes spat back at him, for a moment
they appeared mouldy green, so much so that he wanted
to wipe them clean with his towel, and that full of smoke;
incense burning, the smell of weed, all of this before the
rationalisation that we borrowed everything from the
Pagans bar sexual freedom; this is the true expression of
desire; why, if he had need to defecate, he defecates; the
need to sing in Latin, he sings … his voice sentimental
like his father, who only wore vests and stank of BO; sees
the tiny stairs to the loft, smells the sweet smell of sweat;
when his father got so close the smell changed to a kind
of dull perfume, Goddamn the thing, it was embedded in
everything, the soft chairs, the bedspread, in the old mat his
mother left by the door.

His father knew about smell and what it did … when
his mother made dinner, the smell of boiling cabbage was
spread by steam; it condensated along cold brick walls till
it ran down to the lino in thin lines; only to leave one thick
drop at the end, and once when he snared a drop on his
finger, it soon drained to nothing, but for ages after his
finger smelled of cabbage. Mirrors, in that house; one was a
half-length mirror on the dresser and when he looked over
his shoulder he saw his own bare bum, and he liked the
look of it, the hard skin and the crack which was circular
like a scythe. His father always made sure that his mother

was at mass ... that was his secret, and it is where secrets were learned and lest he forget it was his father who gave him instruction in English, and it was the priests who taught him Latin.

Imagine a sound of boys' voices chatting in the distance, drowned by the curates barking out orders and the silent hum of adults whispering prayers, this towel stung his eyes so much so that he had to reverse it and wet it, to relieve the stinging pain. The boys were getting closer; they were by the door and he was glad the door was big-framed and heavy-duty; it was locked and the knocking started and whilst he fixed his vestments, he ignored it; he returned to the dull side of the mirror and it suddenly and brutally showed the truth, his hair was stuck to the side of his head like steel wool, so he prays and then thinks he is St Francis and then he thinks he is St Paul ... the knocking continues, sharper and more urgent.

'Yes, yes ... I am coming, we have all of the day.'

The boy says, 'Father Mulhern is waitin on you, Father Morris!'

This boy looks at him, his mouth gaping, his altar boy frock is dirty where he spilled food on it, but it is the boy behind him that stands out as he is much younger, but taller, and has filled out with a kind touch of yellow to pale his skin and a girls' mouth that pouts with such richness he possibly stole all from a child's doll.

'Tell Father Mulhern we still have a good half hour; I will be along in a minute ... now run along ...' The gaping

boy leaves and the other boy goes to follow but Father
Morris stops him with his left hand.

'I need you to help me lift a box ... what are you called?'

'Simon, Father.'

Father Morris hesitates so the boy, smiling, says, 'Simon
Byrne, Father ... you know me da, he is in the choir.'

'Byrne,' Father Morris pretends to ponder whilst closing
the door and then inspects the boy, who stands awkwardly.

'Where in Sallynoggin are you from?'

'We live in Sallynoggin Park, Father, over by the pitches.'

'Right.' Father Morris moves back to the basin and the
mirror, leaving the boy standing fidgeting. He picks up the
soapy towel and drops it into the wicker laundry basket.
But the good side of the mirror pains him once more and
it isn't true to say that he has never done this before, is it
why he has no desire now ... whatever had amused him
has dissipated; he wants to tell the boy to go away and that
he has changed his mind, and that he doesn't need his assistance any longer, but instead he says, 'Do you like Corpus
Christi, Simon?'

'I don't understand it, Father.'

'What ... you don't understand it?'

'No, Father ... like, I know we march through the
parish like ... all of us walkin the streets till we get to the
football field, and the benediction like ...'

'Do you know when I was young I didn't understand it
either; in the town where I lived we marched from one end
of the main street to the other; men women and children
and a few priests, it always made a fine spectacle; but sure I
would have as soon been hitting a sliother over the goalposts

as saying prayers, hah?' Father Morris turns around to face the boy, who is standing nervously, he having the look of a fellow who badly needs something to lean on.

The boy remains uneasy; he is silent and respectful, awaiting instruction.

'To be honest, Simon; it was the worst of days ... I was a great Catholic as a boy, I loved all of the ceremony ... everything about the liturgy, I loved my priests their vestments, the serenity ... the way they raised the wafer containing the body and blood of Jesus Christ ... Do you think the body and blood of Jesus Christ is in the wafer, Simon?'

The boy goes red.

'I dunno, Father, you are sayin words like I don't understand them ... I have to go and meet my brother, he is waitin for me on the church steps ... he is only small ...'

'The church steps,' Father Morris walks to the end of room and pulls the drapes, which allow a shaft of light wash the room, leaving the boy blinded temporarily so he puts his hand up over his eye so he can see.

'Do you think God made that sun?'

The boy is bemused now, 'I think that God made everythin ... isn't that right, Father?'

The axe fell on the block of wood and it was so perfect, the dust so fine. His father was an expert, and how the inside of a block of wood was just as he imagined, and then he wondered had he dreamed of it or had he just seen it many times before ... but maybe he just didn't want to remember. Some of the wood was sappier than the rest, and he remembered his mother saying things about children crying and that some kids just cried for the sake of it, and his father added that some children in his time cried because they went to bed hungry, so then they would start an argument, his father going on about how the Church built their cathedrals on the backs of the poor; but she defended the Church stoutly, saying that God deserved the grandeur, sure aren't we eternally grateful for the world he has given us? They ended the argument in silence and she left to walk down the town and visit the church and pray, Father chopping wood, making him watch as the axe fell and the wet wood cracked.

'Do you like our church, Simon, do you think it's a nice building?'

'It's the best, Father ... you are not forgetting about my brother?'

'I was an only child ... no brothers or sisters ... my mother was very religious but my father was a Pagan ... You didn't think your parish priest was the son of a Pagan now, did you?'

'We learned about Pagans at school, Father. I don't think I want to be a Pagan.'

'No, no ... but maybe the Pagans were right to worship the sun ... but sure look it's alright now ... I don't need a hand to lift a box after all ... You had best go to meet your brother, he will get tired of waiting for you.'

'Thanks, Father.'

'Goodbye, Simon.'

The boy struggles to open the heavy door and he eases it closed. Father Morris follows him, locking it once again, and the sun finds a cloud and the room is suddenly cast with shadows.

The axe splitting the wood and the smell of sweat; before the dust darted to corners on the narrow stairs. His father standing over him, the big powerful man with massive muscles, complete with a dazed look and two lazy eyes, this simple angular reflection of his own body ... and his father continually stroking his head ... the power of mathematics, set through a cruciality of angles ... He wanted to kiss that power but the moment hurtled past, his great mind was now impotent, oh father my teacher, oh teacher my father ...

Soon he would lead his flock, his congregation of flesh, followers who will march solemnly behind him along the streets where they live ... passing their own desolate gardens, they will review the grey stone ... beyond those steel walls where they hide, cows and pigs once grazed, and they will continue to make animal noises as people pass. The boy Simon could have been his; it was his first venture into power so why he didn't, and why on Corpus Christi of all days has this made it even worse?

Why had he refused to give in ...? Was he just post-poning the great event, pushing it further down the line, he imagines places and then he sees the faces of different children ... yes, that is all he has done, pushed it further down the line; it will happen, it is only a matter of when, he concludes that he only did what he did out of the fear of discovery; the gods had instructed him; they had marked him out as a man above the animals and that was it, he was the victim of the sun gods, who had feasted on his integrity.

Soon Father Mulhern will come knocking at the door and he will fluster and shout, calling out for his parish priest, who has been chopping wood, taking the wet sap from the interior to spread across the red of his chin ... the cure chopped wood sap. There will follow a silence and then the jangle of keys and a forced entrance.

'Are you alright, Father? ... The church is full, we need to begin mass.' He could hear the pleading moaning whine of his curate. Mass indeed, get out the Monstrance, so as the parish priest can lead his flock along the open road ... We can gaze at the bleeding host, 'Let it bleed on humanity; let it drip blood on the poverty, may we have a collection ... let's go to Rome and give these poor people their money back ...'

Then comes the loud knocking, followed by the fluster, yet his mind is engaging the innocent children, as his father pats his head, and he sees his own bottom, it with a deep crevice ... in the mirror on the dresser ... and the boy, feeling a chill, waits on the church steps for his older brother.

Leaving

1968

The wind is biting into my throat; I turn and look at the Marian statue and the black railing surrounding it makes me feel like I'm in prison. I watch the boys – they are running up and down the hill, then tire and go on to the bike shed; they make screeching noises, wading in a constant hum. Brother Markey walks in straight lines up and down the yard, stops to speak to a master who leans against the wall beside the entrance door but the master has the look of a fellow who agrees to do something and then changes his mind, his whole demeanour says this. The Brother says something funny to him but he just smiles; the master can't bring himself to laugh.

I watch as Brother Markey keeps on going till he completes his journey and he looks at more black railings leading out to the narrow street where a steady trickle of cars go by. He is a sentry. He does an about turn and the waders separate for him, magically the magnificent hum lowers and boys take their eyes away from whatever they are at, just to look at him, and make sure that he passes. When he reaches the master this time, he chooses to ignore him as maybe he is sensing that any engagement would be a waste of time.

He makes his way slowly down by the wall to where Brown and I stand. I am about to say something to Brown, who is docile, pulling at the collar of his coat to keep his throat warm, just like his mother has told him to do. Markey pounces; he grabs this skinhead kid; the boy is stunned, he flaps like a stranded fish, making no effort to move whilst Brother Markey squeezes the blood from his right arm. The waders go quiet; all of the games have stopped and the hum is no longer.

'Look at 'im!' says the Brother. 'He had his arm in a coat pocket.'

The master reluctantly leaves the wall and he makes his way down. Markey points to the duffel coat hanging on the railing; its owner is down by the bike shed playing football.

'Did he take anythin?' the master asks.

'Didn't get a chance,' Brother Markey says.

'I caught 'im red handed!'

'What would you expect!' the master says. 'He is one of the Dwyers – been stealin since he could walk.'

Brother Markey, squeezing his arm harder, drags him away from the wall; taking out his leather strap, he then pulls the boy's arm out so that his hand is straight. Markey hits him three unmerciful blows, then he grabs his other hand and does the same. The boy doesn't flinch. Markey goes red in the face, he says, 'If I see you at it again yer gone from here.' The boy shows no emotion – he walks off up the yard like he feels no pain. I watch him till he disappears amongst the crowd. I want to talk about it with Brown but he is still miserable with his throat. He clutches his collar, and he won't let go.

'You can't hold it all day.'

'It will be warmer inside,' he says, 'me ma told me not to get cold.'

'She's right,' I say. 'Yer man Dwyer is tough, isn't he?'

'Tough as they come – I would be cryin wit the pain of it!'

'Yeah, he don't give a shite, feels nuthin, wish I could be like that.'

Brown looks at me, 'Yer not like him.'

'I know dat!'

The bell rings and the boys run to form a queue at the door – but the master pushes the fellas at the front back. 'Get back in line!' he screams. 'I will get you later, Madden,' he addresses one of the A class, a big tall fella who just laughs. The master ignores him because he is a brilliant hurler and footballer and our school hasn't won anything for years.

Below the stairs there is a smell of coal although there hasn't been coal down there for a long time. When we reach the top we turn right; we pass by the framed photos of the gallant men of 1916 – Brown is in front of me. I follow him to our desk by the window.

Our master is drinking water; he turns his back on us momentarily, then suddenly swivels. He says, 'I got a new a series of Ladybirds for you fellas.'

The fellas he refers to come from old side of town – three of them, but the master has only two copies of *Peter and Jane*. Martin Tate reads, 'Peter and Jane go to the shop. Jane says ...'

I am bored now. I wonder does he have any new books for the class library as the last time I got *Biggles Flies South*. I was hoping the master might get *Biggles Buries the Hatchet*. I had seen the title listed on the 'other titles by this author' page.

I hear the sound of the milk crates banging out in the hall and the door opens. The handsome, red-haired woman traipses up the aisle quietly, giving each boy a half pint of milk and a bun; sometimes it is a waiting game as it depends on where you sit as to how many buns she has left; she passes the boys reading from *Peter and Jane*; it is John Turner now and I see she has five buns left so I count and it should reach me. I miscounted, though, and it stops at Brown. He looks at the bun for a moment, then passes it to me. Brown doesn't speak for if the master catches you talking he will beat you. I imagine the orange cover of *Biggles Flies South*, how it wooed me when I first saw it.

Turner is finishing, 'Jane says ...'

And it's David Evans' turn. He starts off, 'Peter a – and Jan-e go to da sh-op.' The master goes to stand beside him, ready to pounce if there is any deliberate slacking. Satisfied there isn't, he moves away again as Evans says, 'Jan-e and Pe – ter.'

I hear the class next door sing, 'Hail Queen of Heaven, the ocean star ...' I see the bright star shine on the green ocean and I am pleased there is a Queen of Heaven and then I wish that I was in the A class as they have a young Christian Brother – he brings in a guitar; he teaches them songs; they sing hymns every day. The master is back at the top of the classroom – he turns his back again and Turner, bowing his big head, asks Tate can he have his bun. Tate says no, he is bringing it home, then Turner tells Tate to shove it up his hole; the master turns round, races over and slaps Turner across the head, 'You're illiterate – but you still have a mouth on you!'

'Sorry, sur, I was lookin for an extra bun,' Turner pleads.

The master is ready to slap him over the head again. He looks around for the leather strap he normally keeps on his desk, but then he says, 'Gerard Brown, you look very pale.'

Brown tries to smile but it's lost within him. 'Have a bad throat, sir.'

All the fellas at the front turn sharply to check him out, 'Maybe a drink of water, Gerard – it might be a help?'

'I might be alright sir, me ma said I was to watch it.'

'She is right, son, a bad throat is a bugger.'

The class next door are off again; their voices lend a lilt to the air and I'd swear it cheers the master so he leaves Turner be and he goes to the blackboard, where he picks up some chalk and starts to write. I am thinking, why does the master treat Turner one way and Gerard Brown another? Then Tate gives Turner his bun – he looks around, laughing, and Turner promises he will beat the crap out of him in the Tech lane after school. The master is writing words on the board; they are big words that I never heard of.

'Does anyone know the meaning of any of these words?'

Brown says, 'I think I know what an acronym is, sir.' The master holds the chalk high, his hand in the air like he wants to start writing on the board again.

'USA, sir, that's an acronym for United States of America.'

The master, smiling at Gerard, goes back to his blackboard but he turns around again, he shouts, 'By God, Brown, I don't know why they lumped you in with these idiots.' He points deliberately at Turner and Tate.

The music stops next door and the master reads some of the other words he has written. He wants to know if anyone save for Brown knows what they mean; I know one word, 'lotus', and just like he is reading my mind he picks my word. I want to put up my hand but I don't and nobody does. I know the answer, as we have Scalextric, and one of the cars is a Lotus. It's funny as I feel a sense of excitement even though I am not going to say anything. I look over to the far row, where the brainy boys are; I look at the O'Connor twins and then Kevin Reid, but they stay quiet like they are afraid to give the wrong answer.

'Anyone?' the master looks down at the O'Connors.

I mumble under my breath – well he points at me, forgetting my name.

'Dunno sir.'

'Thought you knew the answer, no?'

'No sir.'

I want to say it out, 'It's a racing car,' but I just can't, the words won't leave my lips.

'It's a flower, you gombeens!' he says and then rubs all of his words out in frustration, the duster sending smoke up to the ceiling.

*

It's wet along Sussex Street, the rain filling dark pools under parked cars, their bonnets holding tanks of soft water dripping onto moulded rubber wheels. Brown usually runs but his throat doesn't allow – so for once I am glad; I don't need to run after him.

Sussex Street is busy with boys, some running and some walking in groups. I see my reflection in the dark window of the bookmaker's, then I lose it in the bright lights of the Lido café. On the main street people are dodging the rain; oul wans are spraying umbrellas dangerously; the number eight bus passes, splashing buckets of water onto the footpath. Brown wants to go into Dixon's to get a ruler but I want to go into Woollies to get pick'n'mix. The guy behind the counter smokes a cigar, he chuckles at the wet hands that beseech him for service – he is out of rulers, he will have them in on Friday – we go back out into the rain and shuffle on the few yards to Woolworths; they have broken biscuits with pieces of Fry's chocolate cream and vats of smarties; its pick'n'mix with liquorish allsorts. Brown has only six pence and his bus fare but I have a shilling and my fare so I sub him and the pretty girl serving smiles at us; I like her smile but Brown doesn't notice her at all. Back on the street the wind blows; the rain stinging our faces, we wait in the queue outside Doyle's shop.

Two fat oul wans are hogging the space by the bus stop – one is telling the other to reel her daughter in, she says, 'It wudn't be happenin on mi watch, Sissy!'

Sissy is quiet now; she is thinking of something very precious. 'I know she is a dreadful worry.'

The other oul wan shouts, 'Keep her in, Sissy, dat's wat I'd do, keep her fuckin in!'

Sissy looks down the street towards St Michael's Hospital, she is hoping for a bus, one comes but it is too far away to see the number; the whole queue looks on; it's another number 8 and it splashes by.

Then two 7a's come together, which is good because the first one is fairly full and the oul wans get on and go downstairs. The conductor blocks us, using his elbow. 'The one behind,' he shouts; all of the folk behind us sigh and the older contingent examine the second bus nervously.

The rain is falling in sheets now and the second bus is only half full. The conductor is a young chap, who jumps off to lift on a buggy; he takes care folding it and puts it in the space under the stairs. Brown and I go upstairs, which is three-quarters full. Some young ones from the Dominican convent are throwing rolled-up balls of paper at each other. Brown lets me have the window seat and I rub the cold glass vigorously with the sleeve of my coat. I manage to remove the steam but still the rain restricts my view to a mass of tiny bubbles. The bus has screeching brakes and the driver stops to chat with a comrade coming the other way; this old man sitting opposite throws his eyes to Heaven, then he takes out a Sweet Afton and lights it up. The smokes drifts above our heads and I know why they call the fags Sweet Afton as there was something warm and appetising about the smell. The bus moves on and Brown moves uncomfortably, trying to settle himself because, like me, his trousers are sticking with the damp and all has become too tight.

We pass the church and on down the main street and the bus screeches to a halt once more; outside Lee's Furniture Store a crowd gathers. A banner says, 'Grand Opening Lee's Furniture Store'; women appear from everywhere followed by servile men with their heads bowed, and Gay Byrne lauds it over the rabble – a tall man in a suit tries to protect him with an umbrella and the whole left aisle are on their feet. The old man sticks the Sweet Afton into his mouth as he hovers over us and all of the time he is wiping the window so as he can get a better view. The girls from the Dominican convent lower the fly window, 'Howya Gay,' a curly-headed girl shouts; a scrawny young one screams, 'Cum on, Gay – give us a wave!' Her voice is lost amidst the passing traffic and the noise of the crowd.

The conductor arrives. 'Close that fuckin winda, will yah,' and the scrawny girl just looks at him defiantly. 'The oul wans will get a soakin!' the young conductor shouts. We move on as Gay and his entourage move indoors out of the rain.

The bus swings right at the end of the main street; the scrawny girl, still standing, falls over onto her seat; the curly headed girl laughs; the scrawny girl says, 'Fuck off, you,' then she laughs too and she decides to sit down properly.

'Fares pleas',' the young conductor asks and Brown pays him; the conductor turns the handle of the ticket machine and the small thin paper ticket emerges.

'Huz yer da?' The young conductor presses the rubber line above his head and then he eyes the mirror at the top of the stairs.

'He is goin to Jervis Street. I think he will be comin home for a day or two!' The young conductor leans over to take my fare. 'Tell 'im Sammy wus askin for 'im.' He gives me my change and then he gives Brown back his fare. 'Tell 'im we want 'im back, de lads all miss 'im.'

And he goes up the aisle; the bus roars its way up to Clengara, then starts to climb the Noggin Hill. The engine roars. I am looking at the high walls that line the road; they guard remote houses and gardens with big trees that shade all beyond them, one wall has cuts of glass embedded at the top and on the other side there is just a line of withered apple trees.

We reach the brow of the hill. The bus stops and Brown starts humming a tune and for the life of me I can't place it; he continues as we pass the old cottages on the right and the slicker bungalows on the left – this is the old Noggin. The bus stops at the Thatch pub I can see men standing at the bar through the narrow windows – they are eager-looking

and red-faced – one of them is looking at the bus to see if
he recognises any of the passengers, but like me the rain
obscures his view; soon Brown stops humming the tune and
the bus turns left at Honeypark and sets off by the factories
Stroud Reilly, then the Rayon Mills. Our Lady of Victories
stands high on the hill, dominating the whole landscape;
and before me the tough grey terraced and semi-d's; and
others are upstairs/downstairs flats.

'What's that yer wer hummin?'

'Dunno the name,' Brown says.

'I know it – it's drivin me mad,' I say back.

'The minute you walked in the joint,' he says.

'I know it,' I say.

'My ma sings it,' Brown says and we leave it that; passing
the church now and the shops facing it; we pass the field
where the itinerants camp each summer, then the big green,
and more houses opposite the gaps. The bus turns tight left
at the Pigs Fields, the hundred yards to the terminus where
we live. Brown says, 'See you,' before crossing the road; the
old man lights another Sweet Afton as he heads away and
the rain has stopped suddenly. It is almost dark. I watch
him walk on under an early street lamp.

*

Brown thinks it's funny that we are both staying in; his ma
has to go to Jervis Street to see his da. My ma has to go into
town to the shops. Staying in is nothing much; you either

bring a packed lunch or you go to the Lido for chips – I don't
mind because it's Thursday and the week is nearly done – I
bring a packed lunch because I don't like chips in the middle
of the day. Chips are night food, but Brown offers me one
and I don't take it as I didn't share my egg-and-tomato sandwiches with him, he didn't ask and I didn't give. The chips
are steaming as we walk down Sussex Street and go right
down Eblana Ave, our schoolyard on our left. The yard is
quiet as most boys go home for lunch and those that don't
are down in the bike shed sheltering from the misty rain.

'James McDonald did his leg in on the spikes at the
Marine Hotel,' Brown says.

'It wasn't his leg, it was his foot,' I say.

Brown looks at me, eating the last of his chips; they're
only half-chips now, the bits that have broken off bigger
chips. We turn down Marine Road by the Elphin Hotel
and I can see the sea now; it's all grey and choppy, the
yachts moored in the harbour are angry with it and they
try to fight the swell. We cross the road, heading past the
Pavilion Cinema.

'Which do you prefer, the Pave or the Adelphi?'

'The Pave is better,' I say, not thinking of any good
reason why.

'I like the Adelphi – my Aunt Tess brought me to see
Snow White, you know, first picture an all dat?'

'Yeah the Pave shows better films though, nuthin like
it,' I say, 'a Palm Grove choc ice; a good film; that's if old
Flemin don't chase you out!' Brown laughs at me.

The seafront has its own smell, with the sea adding to the mixture of plants and bushes lining the railings by the footpath, the damp sea air spreading through all aided ably by the whistling wind. We anticipate the passing trains that hurtle by unseen, below ground, delivering us addictive whiffs of diesel oil. When we reach the entrance to the East Pier a salted wind wets our insides percutaneously and a few older people walk by the higher wall; we choose to walk by the water soes that way we can see the mullet. We get to watch from close range, the breeze tossing the small boats, and Brown looks at the sea and then the sky; he is checking the reflection to see if it's true – he searches the dark water for clouds, a jagged edge; this huge gush of seawater comes from the outer wall and it runs to the bandstand and we race on to get a closer look. The upper level is soaked as the sea lashes it angrily; it floods the concrete slabs and suddenly they are made of sponge. Some of the older people turn back but Brown and I watch as the foam spills over onto the lower level. The yachts are furious, they heave-ho, empty; all grey and cold.

Brown says, 'We best head back – it's a quarter to –'

'Alright.' I am relieved the storm is picking up, the air is heavy away at the end of the pier, the clouds split to allow a piercing light that continues razor-sharp through the mountainous sea; I imagine it as a laser drill.

'Me da was home,' Brown says casually.

'How is he?'

'Not good.'

Brown quickens the pace. He worries we will be late back and the master will flail us. I catch up with him as we pass the yacht club. We cross the road to walk by the railway; a train passes and the ground shakes – the tremor doesn't frighten us, we just don't like the deafening sound.

'I heard him and me ma talkin, he was sayin that he was leavin us. I could see them plain as day, the bedroom door was open.'

'Did they see you?'

'Nah, come on,' Brown runs across Marine Road and we walk by the town hall and the post office.

'He said he was leavin and she started to beat his chest with her fists; me da just stood there and took it until my ma sort of ran out of energy and she just collapsed on him and then he just hugged her like she was a child.'

We turn into Eblana Avenue and boys are running into the yard, it's five to two. Brother Markey stands at the gate to intimidate stragglers; he smiles at Brown, who looks at his watch and smiles back gratefully, and I pass by under the cover of Brown.

'He is gone now,' Brown says as we climb the stairs. 'Yeh know he never told me or the girls he was leavin; he only told me ma!'

We reach the classroom and the master is drinking water and Turner whispers to Tate, who then whispers to Evans; he says that he pissed in the cup when the master went out for a minute. Tate believes the story but Evans doesn't really but he is laughing anyway. The master, sensing something is afoot, turns, suddenly glaring at the motley crew; he hands Tate a Ladybird book, and then, very slowly, he issues Turner and Evans one between them. Tate starts to read but he chokes to get a word. It is an easy word and Brown whispers it just loud enough for Tate to hear: 'where'. Brown whispers again; the master looks at him but he doesn't do anything. Tate still can't say it, he is getting flustered with the master towering over him.

He stops altogether and the master shouts, 'I can't teach you nothing if yeh can't read the word "where"!' Evans starts to laugh and so does Turner – the master lashes out, hits Tate across the back of the head. It's a big slap and both of the O'Connors wince. Tate sticks his head into the book in an effort to concentrate, but the master, frustrated, hits him again; this time Evans is engulfed with laughter so the master hits him a clatter and then, seeing Turner's head bopping, he gives him an unmerciful blow. Turner's head hits the desk. Tate goes 'where', but the master isn't done as he catches Evans on the side of the face and his rodent-like cheek fills up red; Tate starts to sob, which prompts Evans to do likewise. Turner won't cry – he just stares at the master like he is waitin for something – the master goes back to his desk and he sits quietly for moment. Tate sobs the loudest, while Evans sobs but with the sound turned down.

I look out the window and Brown just fiddles with his pencil; the sky is closing and the blinds are half drawn; outside the rain trickles; it reminds me of that great hunger I feel early in the morning when I long for something hot to eat. The door wraps twice; Brother Markey pokes his head in and the master rushes to attend to him. Markey whispers something into the master's ear and Tate still sobs.

A large lady appears suddenly. I can smell her perfume from my desk. She is tall with blue hair with glued curls – she is pale; she examines the faces like she is looking for someone. 'My Aunt Tess,' Brown says, and his aunt beckons him to come; she doesn't smile. Brown gathers his things.

'What's up?'

He looks at me like I have gone mad. 'Me da is gone.' The master hands him his overcoat, he mutters, 'Thanks, sir,' and he leaves with the perfume still lingering for a few moments.

It's funny waiting for the bus without Brown; he is always there, now suddenly I am missing him. I lean against Doyle's window, I allow the oul wans squabble with the kids; the bus is full, the conductor is hassled. He shouts, 'One along in a few minutes!' He rings the bell angrily. The bus takes off – it leaves the stranded oul wans and kids smarting, and I wonder what all the fuss is about; there will be other buses, we will all get home, it's just a matter of when. The evening is dark and the lights go on, the next bus comes down the street, illuminated, and I get on with the regular girls from the Dominican convent. They look subdued. I follow them upstairs, seeing the smooth white skin of their calves as they climb, but I feel relieved they go sit at the front. I stay at the back. Along the pavement people still shuffle; outside McCullaghs an old woman has fallen and there is a sudden crowd around her. For some reason the traffic queues coming up Marine Road.

The journey is lonely. I feel isolated and victimised without my pal and I wonder what it is like when someone leaves you and in your head you know that you will never see them again. Turning that dark corner to climb the Noggin Hill to find yourself confronted by all those houses, these are the property of dolls. Will Brown's da be just the first, and will all of the other da's die too? What's the point of having a da?

The bus winds its way noisily, turning the sharp left by the Pigs Fields; I hop off. The people carry their shopping bags and lift their prams. The grass in the ring is wet, it sticks to my shoes. I wish it was summer as nobody seems to die in summer. The rain has stopped and the gardens and hedges are washed; the paths are stained but soon they will dry back to brilliant white. The bus pulls away and I see Brown's older sister as she fixes a sign to the front door. I wonder what it says and I can't very well go over and ask.

I am glad to open the front door of my house and inhale the familiar homely smell. I feel the damp drip from me whilst hanging my coat on the bannister. Yeah, I think of summer, the trips to the baths, the football matches we will play in the ring, will this keep Brown going? I wonder what he is doing now. Maybe he is sitting by the fire bewildered, whilst his mother hands him cups of tea – maybe not, perhaps he wants me to call by with a ball. Maybe he needs a distraction. I picture the faces: first his, then his oldest sister and then the youngest, lastly his ma. They are so alone now.

The rain starts again. It lashes the tiny window panels by the front door and I sit four steps up on the stairs so as I can see out. The terminus is empty, not a person waits for a bus and the rain beats the road, the tiny streams search for drains and a car pulls up; Brown's Aunt Tess and a man and another woman get out. They walk slowly to the front door; the man holds an umbrella up over the women and Browns' front door opens slowly and they go in.

The door remains open for a minute, then it finally closes; it is time to shake myself up. I go to the living room and turn on the television, the presenter is making jokes and then it goes to ads. I survey the living room and I am thankful and I wish that it will stay this way forever and never change. I am feeling momentarily warm.